BEST
DETECTIVE
FICTION

BEST
DETECTIVE
FICTION

A guide from Godwin to the present

MELVYN BARNES

CLIVE BINGLEY
LONDON

&

LINNET BOOKS
HAMDEN · CONN

FIRST PUBLISHED 1975 BY CLIVE BINGLEY LTD
16 PEMBRIDGE ROAD LONDON W11
SIMULTANEOUSLY PUBLISHED IN THE USA BY LINNET BOOKS
AN IMPRINT OF THE SHOE STRING PRESS INC
995 SHERMAN AVENUE HAMDEN CONNECTICUT 06514

SET IN 10 ON 12 POINT BASKERVILLE
PHOTOSET PRINTED AND BOUND
IN GREAT BRITAIN BY
REDWOOD BURN LIMITED
TROWBRIDGE & ESHER

Library of Congress Cataloguing in Publication Data

Barnes, Melvyn P
Best detective fiction.

     Bibliography: p.
     Includes index.
     1. Detective and mystery stories—History and criticism. I. Title.
PN3448.D4B3.   823'.0872   75–22344
ISBN 0–208–01376–8 (Linnet Books)

Contents

For Jeremy William
and Timothy Edmund

Preface

The creation of this bibliography has been to some extent a matter of personal preferences. Although at least half of the books included are held by most authorities to be key contributions to the genre, there are others which might provoke disagreement from among the vast army of detective fiction enthusiasts. Similarly it includes some authors who are too recent to have been put in perspective among their fellow crime writers, and it may transpire that their 'best' books are yet to come; alternatively, like so many bestselling authors of the twenties and thirties, they may not survive the test of time, and in any future compilation of this kind all mention of their works might be expunged.

A need has existed for a work of this nature. Although several excellent historical surveys of detective fiction have appeared, together with some volumes of criticism, they have concentrated upon the development of the form rather than bibliographical considerations. The librarian, the researcher, and of course the detective story addict will find listed the acknowledged classics. In addition many authors of the past twenty years, if they have made significant contributions, are represented by works which will serve as good introductions to their styles and techniques for readers who might not have sampled them before.

At this point a word regarding the basis of selection is necessary.

Firstly, the word *best* must be defined. Each selected title fulfils one or more of the following criteria: excellence of plot, writing and/or characterisation, or a degree of innovation which has established or enhanced a trend. There are therefore thousands of detective stories which have found no place here; in common with all branches of literature, the field has produced many examples which are mediocre, unoriginal or bad. A further criterion has been brought into play in a minority of cases – sheer durability, in that public demand has been sustained to an extent which marks the works concerned as something exceptional.

Secondly, how has the term *detective fiction* been defined? This has been a far more difficult problem, as the generally loose employment of the term has frequently covered not only the classic puzzle form, but also action thrillers, suspense novels, spy stories, and so on *ad infinitum*. In the present case a distinction has been drawn between detective fiction and thrillers. The thriller, which may indeed have a detective as its central character, relies for its effect upon pace and action, and the question posed is 'what is going to happen next?' or 'how will the hero get out of a fix?' Thus to give but two examples, the novels of Leslie Charteris and John Creasey have been excluded, although Creasey's more realistic work as 'J J Marric' is quoted. Spy stories have similarly been excluded.

Nevertheless there are some works included here which are not written in the classic puzzle form. To suit the present purpose they can be defined as detective fiction for want of a better term – crime fiction, as an alternative, sounds too broad. Mainly they are works in which the identity of the criminal is not concealed from the reader, and indeed is revealed in some cases on the first page. Sometimes the criminal is the narrator and his thought processes are thus laid bare. They qualify for inclusion mainly because they are a logical extension of a literary form which, at times in its history, has displayed signs of becoming tired. A detective novel which poses the questions *why?* or *how?* is considered no less appropriate than one which asks *who?* In many of these cases the reader is in possession of all the evidence before the detective appears, and yet there is still a puzzle element involved in deducing how the detective will establish the criminal's guilt. In other cases no actual detective appears, and it must be appreciated that this absence does not invalidate a detective story – here the word is interpreted in its adjectival sense. To have eliminated from this bibliography, on purist grounds, the works of such masters as Francis Iles would have destroyed the effect of well roundedness which it is hoped has been achieved.

Regarding citation, each title is listed in its first edition in the English language, and also its first British edition if different; place of publication is London unless otherwise stated. It is hoped that this will be of value to collectors as well as to librarians, and in fact to the general reader who wishes to use it as a recommended reading list. All pseudonymous works, which represents a large proportion of the field in question, are cited under the pseudonym, although actual names are mentioned in the text when appropriate.

It must be emphasised that this volume is not intended as a complete history of detective fiction, even though its narrative form and the general arrangement of related titles combine to give a superficial picture of the development of the genre. There are already several analytico-historical accounts which have been invaluable to the present writer during twenty years of building the collection of detective fiction upon which this descriptive bibliography is based. They are highly recommended, and that by Julian Symons has been described as the classic study of crime fiction.

Howard Haycraft *Murder for pleasure* New York Appleton-Century 1941; Peter Davies 1942

Ellery Queen *Queen's quorum: a history of the detective-crime short story* Boston Little, Brown 1951; Gollancz 1953

A E Murch *The development of the detective novel* Peter Owen 1958

Tage la Cour and Harald Mogensen *The murder book* Allen & Unwin 1971

Eric Quayle *The collector's book of detective fiction* Studio Vista 1972

Julian Symons *Bloody murder* Faber 1972 and Penguin 1974

Finally, an invitation is extended to anyone who either disagrees with the inclusion of an individual item, or alternatively feels that a worthwhile item has been excluded. Do please make your views known.

Melvyn Barnes

1 From the beginnings

The detective story as we know it dates from 1841 with the first publication of Poe's *The murders in the Rue Morgue*, but various authorities have observed elements of detection in the literature of a far earlier age. Examples have been quoted from the Apocryphal scriptures concerning the exploits of Daniel, from Virgil's *Aeneid*, from Herodotus, and from Chaucer's *Canterbury tales*. In each of these works there are puzzles presented, some involving crime, and solutions are reached by the crude employment of some of the techniques which detective novelists of the twentieth century were to enhance with the elaborations of our modern age.

It must nevertheless be stressed that there is no clear intention in any of these early works to present a detective story in the sense that readers have now come to understand the term. Their interest to the crime fiction enthusiast or historian is, one would have thought, purely academic. They are therefore excluded from this bibliography, together with *The Arabian nights entertainments* and Voltaire's *Zadig*. Also excluded are the works of the picaresque novelists, the gothic novelists, Fenimore Cooper, Balzac, Eugène Sue and Dumas. The extent to which such writers employed the techniques of detective fiction is a fascinating study in itself, and interested readers are referred to the books quoted in the preface, particularly the study by A E Murch.

Mention must be made, however, of two key works which had much influence on the literature that was to come. Considerably predating Poe, but so important that they must be cited in this bibliography as the earliest examples of pure detection, were the works of Godwin and Vidocq.

William Godwin (1756–1836), philosopher and atheist, wrote
GODWIN William
Things as they are; or, the Adventures of Caleb Williams
Three volumes
B Crosby 1794
primarily as a propagandist novel, but contained within it is a classic of detective fiction involving a murder and an amateur detective who

11

identifies the criminal by the analysis of clues which the author has deliberately contrived. Generally known by its subtitle, it may be defined as a gothic romance, although not one that is specially remembered today. Godwin set out to demonstrate the need for social and political reform rather than to tell a straightforward story of murder and its consequences, and of course the term 'detective story' was not at that time in common usage. The tyranny of rich landlords, the abuse of power by the few in authority, and the wretchedness of the penal system: all were depicted here by Godwin before ever Dickens came on the scene, and the pity of it is that Godwin's chief claim to fame today is that his daughter created Frankenstein.

Furthermore Godwin's propaganda is in no sense obtrusive, even if we are considering the novel as the earliest piece of detective fiction. Caleb Williams investigates the murder of an obnoxious landlord for which two tenants have been hanged, and discovers that his own employer is guilty. In order to do this Williams uses methods which were later adopted by countless investigators in the field of which Poe became the acknowledged founder. Following his successful enquiries, Williams is hounded by the murderer through a series of adventures involving prison, various disguises, and numerous scenes depicting the gaping social inequalities of the age. The theme of the pursuer pursued has been subsequently used by scores of thriller writers, as has Godwin's technique (described in his preface) of planning the story backwards. As an example of propagandist fiction, as a picaresque novel, or as the first pure detective story, this work merits further study today.

When Godwin was writing *Caleb Williams*, much of his research into the activities of criminals was conducted with the aid of *The Newgate calendar*. These annals of the gaol wherein resided (in many instances for short periods pending execution) the most notorious villains as well as the saddest cases of degraded humanity, provided material for many novelists of the picaresque school. In some cases the pursuit of the criminal, as narrated in *The Newgate calendar*, involved something approaching detective work, but it was not until the publication of Vidocq's memoirs that latent writers of detective fiction were provided with accounts of authentic criminal investigation of a kind which could inspire them.

Eugène François Vidocq (1775–1857) was the first head of the Paris Sûreté and later a private detective. At the outset of his career, however, he was the hunted rather than the hunter. His progression from criminal to detective was to be reflected in such fictional characters as Gaboriau's Lecoq, Leblanc's Arsène Lupin, and Chesterton's Flambeau.

VIDOCQ Eugène François
Memoirs of Vidocq, principal agent of the French Police until 1827
Four volumes
Hunt 1828–1829

is included in this bibliography of best detective fiction in spite of its apparently factual status, because there is little doubt that it was heavily fictionalised and highly coloured. Vidocq was evidently something of a showman, and time and again these memoirs describe techniques and *modus operandi* which now, 150 years later, it is possible to detect in hundreds of novels which have been written in the intervening period. His mastery of the art of disguise, and his knowledge of the lore and language of the underworld, are but two examples of aspects of the 'Great Detective' which anticipated several significant writers of the nineteenth century at least – including Gaboriau and Conan Doyle – who in turn gave rise to the tremendous upsurge of interest in the awakening field which has come to be known as detective fiction.

Although the Paris Sûreté had been established, there was still in the early nineteenth century no force of professional detectives in Britain or in the United States. This has been advanced by some authorities as the reason why detective stories as such could not be written at the time, the argument being that it is not possible to write about things before they exist. Although this argument has much to commend it, the principle does not seem to have worried Jules Verne or H G Wells, who came later. Be that as it may, no professional detectives emerged in fiction until they existed in reality.

The memoirs of Vidocq quite clearly influenced the work of Edgar Allan Poe, who is accepted as the father of the detective story. Poe (1809–1849) was an American who spent his early life in Britain, and who had a tremendous interest in the European scene. After producing some poetry and other literary work which took some years to attract public attention, he realised that the field of fiction was a more likely means of supporting him financially, and furthermore that the short story form was capable of distinct improvement. He became literary editor of *Graham's magazine*, and

13

during his encumbency published *The murders in the Rue Morgue*. This was a cornerstone, a foundation stone even, being the first example of a piece of fiction in which the reader is presented with a detective and a mystery which is not only integral, but is the be-all and end-all of the work. Godwin's novel listed above, for example, used a detective theme within a piece of reformist propaganda, and in Vidocq's work there was scant attention paid to intellectual analysis.

The murders in the Rue Morgue was the first pure detective story, although it is unlikely that Poe thought of it in that light. It also introduced the first great series detective of fiction, the Chevalier C Auguste Dupin. A man 'of an excellent, indeed of an illustrious family', he is something of an intellectual recluse with powers of observation second to none and techniques of deductive reasoning never previously employed in fiction. He therefore possessed advantages which had been denied to Vidocq, as Dupin himself states: "'Vidocq . . . was a good guesser, and a persevering man. But, without educated thought, he erred continually . . .'"

This quotation is further evidence of Poe's familiarity with Vidocq's memoirs. He was also acquainted with the work of French scientists, and clearly researched backgrounds for his detective stories to a degree which some modern writers in the field would do well to emulate. His Paris settings, quite naturally therefore, displayed an authentic atmosphere.

The murders in the Rue Morgue first appeared in the April 1841 issue of *Graham's magazine*. The second Dupin story, *The mystery of Marie Roget*, appeared in *Snowden's ladies companion* in the issues for November and December 1842 and February 1843. The third and last, *The purloined letter*, made its first appearance in *The gift*, an annual dated 1845 but published in the latter part of 1844 by the Philadelphia firm of Carey and Hart. Poe wrote only two more stories which can be classified in the detective canon, *The gold bug* and *Thou art the man*, neither of which featured Dupin. All three Dupin stories, together with *The gold bug*, first appeared together in volume form as

POE Edgar A
Tales
New York and London Wiley & Putnam 1845

which was edited by Evert A Duyckincke, and all five stories appeared in

(POE Edgar A)
The works of the late Edgar Allan Poe: with notices of his life

14

and genius
Three volumes
New York J S Redfield 1850
which was edited by N P Willis and others and is normally described
as the Griswold edition. The rarity of the above volumes means that
collectors probably need to turn to the slightly later collected edition
published in London as
POE Edgar A
Tales of mystery, imagination and humour; and poems
Simms and McIntyre 1852
which is interesting because, as its title suggests, it was the forerunner
of numerous editions of Poe's short stories popularly known as *Tales of
mystery and imagination*, and of course containing the master's many
studies in murder, horror and the supernatural in addition to the
exploits of Auguste Dupin. Modern editions are available in
Everyman's Library (Dent) and World's Classics (OUP).

At this point it may be useful to examine briefly the various features
of Poe's detective tales, for they were the models which inspired
countless others. Only the significant devices will be mentioned. It
would be churlish to summarise the stories themselves, as even now
they hold surprises for new readers. They are not faultless by any
means, and various critics have pinpointed individual flaws and at
times made much of them. These stories are too significant to the field
under discussion for the present writer to indulge in such cleverness.

Firstly, there are the general points. As already mentioned, Dupin
was a man of fantastic intelligence, the first omniscient amateur detective who gave rise to hundreds of successors. He was a walking
brain, one might almost say a 'thinking machine' – the sobriquet
chosen by Jacques Futrelle sixty years later for his Professor Augustus
S F X Van Dusen. Dupin was also a most cultured gentleman, and
again this correlation of common sense and intellectualism – so rare,
perhaps, in twentieth century man – was used to the full by Poe's successors in the field. One can cite, among many, S S Van Dine's creation Philo Vance, who had the attributes of Dupin embellished with a
buffoonery of which Poe would almost certainly have disapproved.
Finally there is Dupin's poor regard for the official police, and the jea-
lousy which the police felt. For Dupin one could substitute Sherlock
Holmes and others.

Passing from Dupin himself, we find that the tales are narrated by
an anonymous friend who set the standard for Conan Doyle's Dr

15

Watson in his awestruck admiration for the detective and in his desire to follow in his master's footsteps. Almost every great detective of the late nineteenth and early twentieth century – extending in fact to the nineteen thirties – had their 'Watsons', their chroniclers, sometimes silly and occasionally but rarely intelligent. They never stole the great detective's thunder, and they originated with Dupin's nameless companion. In the nineteen thirties they began to be regarded as old fashioned, but Poe had established a trend which survived for a century.

Then there are the innovations contained within each of Poe's stories. Dupin's investigation in the Rue Morgue is a case of murder within a sealed room. The 'locked room' murder mystery became a popular technique, exemplified by Gaston Leroux in *The mystery of the yellow room* and in countless tales by the twentieth century master of that art, John Dickson Carr *alias* Carter Dickson.

The murder of Marie Roget, Dupin's second case, is a fictional reconstruction of an actual crime – shades of S S Van Dine, and of numerous others up to Fryn Tennyson Jesse and Meyer Levin. It is also told by means of newspaper reports, proving that the conventional narrative form is not entirely necessary to retain the reader's interest, and this was proved again in Collins' *The moonstone*, Dorothy L Sayers' *The documents in the case*, and so on. A further innovation is that Dupin solves the Roget murder by purely studying reports of the case and thus disclaiming the need to indulge in any physical activity; in other words, he founded the 'armchair detective' syndrome which was to be ably adopted, among many others, by Baroness Orczy's old man in the A B C shop and most notably by Rex Stout's immovable Nero Wolfe.

In *The purloined letter* Dupin demonstrates that the obvious, the commonplace, is the solution most likely to be overlooked. It has been done scores of times since, but rarely so effectively. Chesterton, however, made particularly clever use of the idea in several of his Father Brown stories.

The gold bug is less of a detective story as we know it, and deprived of Dupin's presence, but the basic idea relies upon the deciphering of a code. Again this was an idea of considerable importance in the history of detective fiction, especially to those who delighted in presenting facsimile reproductions of strange ciphers for the delectation of their readers and for contemptuous dismissal by their detectives. Consider, for example, the breaking of *The dancing men* by Sherlock Holmes or

The Moabite cipher which taxes R Austin Freeman's Dr John Thorndyke – the latter being a mixture of the cipher story and the 'most obvious solution', two Poeisms in one!

Finally *Thou art the man* reveals a murderer who has prepared a trail of misleading clues, which has become a favourite device in detective fiction. It also contains the first demonstration of rudimentary ballistic science in respect of rifling marks on bullets. Thirdly the murderer is that phenomenon of so many later stories and novels, the 'least likely person'. The outstanding practitioner of this device is Agatha Christie, and the ultimate example probably *The murder of Roger Ackroyd*.

No apology is made here for devoting so much space to five short stories, the only detective stories Poe wrote. It has been demonstrated, however, that within these five stories are many – if not all – of the basic elements of pure detective fiction. Parallels have been cited, and will appear in their proper chronological context in the following pages. Thus any edition of Poe's stories may be regarded as the detective fiction writer's, or indeed reader's, *vade mecum*. If there had been no C Auguste Dupin, would there still have been a Sherlock Holmes?

2 The pre-Sherlock era

Whether or not one accepts the theory that there could be no detective stories before organised detective forces existed in reality, that particular problem was solved in England in 1842. In that year the Detective Department was established in London, an extremely small body of men destined to be the forefathers of New Scotland Yard. It was therefore only a matter of time before writers turned quite naturally to works of fiction depicting the pursuit and apprehension of criminals by professional detectives.

Poe, although he founded the detective story, provided little immediate inspiration to other writers – particularly in his native America, where there was no impetus whatsoever in the development of detective fiction. The movement was seen more clearly in France and in Britain.

The establishment of the Detective Department was reflected in a spate of fictitious reminiscences published as 'yellow backs', the most notable among many being the pseudonymous 'Waters' created by William Russell and published as

> WATERS
> Recollections of a detective police-officer
> J and C Brown 1856

Perhaps more important was the attention paid to the Detective Department by the novelist Charles Dickens (1812–1870) who embarked upon an early example of the public relations campaign by producing articles in praise of the detectives at a time when public opinion was hostile. No doubt the skulduggery of the Bow Street Runners, who had been superseded, was still fresh in people's minds and the new force had yet to prove itself as honest and impartial. Dickens' participation took the form of articles in *Household words* from July to September 1850, in which he displayed his admiration for one Inspector Field, but more particularly in his novel

> DICKENS Charles
> Bleak House . . . with illustrations by H K Browne
> (Published in parts bound with the wrappers)
> Bradbury & Evans 1853

18

Although the police of the nineteenth century, especially the runners, were characterised in many works of fiction as barely more honest than the villains they pursued, Dickens in *Bleak House* presented a more agreeable, more human image. His 'Inspector Bucket of the Detective' is an amalgam of Field and Vidocq, and the first professional detective to appear in an English novel.

As with all novels by Dickens it can not be neatly categorised, although the author's prime message concerns the costs and delays associated with the Court of Chancery. In the case of Jarndyce and Jarndyce, the estate in dispute is eventually completely absorbed by the costs of the legal action. For the connoisseur of detection, however, the interest lies in the murder of the rascally lawyer Tulkinghorn, for we are then introduced to the methods of the Detective Department. The sharp eyed and kindly Bucket even exposes the murderer to an assembled company of suspects, an innovation which later became almost standard practice in detective novels. Here the detective interest is contained within a major novel by a major novelist and is' remarkable for its faultless characterisation – an attribute too few crime novelists of the twentieth century were to display, but in Dickens' case it borders upon the patronising to mention it.

There are murders and other crimes in many of Dickens' novels, but it was not until

> DICKENS Charles
> The mystery of Edwin Drood . . . with twelve illustrations by S
>   L Fildes, and a portrait
> (Published in parts bound with the wrappers)
> Chapman & Hall 1870

that he came nearest to writing a pure detective story. It was his last book, unfinished at the time of his death. As well as a host of minor Dickensian characters, we are introduced to the sinister John Jasper, precentor of Cloisterham Cathedral. Jasper lives a somewhat schizophrenic existence, alternating respectability with his regular visits to the opium den. His nephew Edwin Drood is betrothed to Rosa Bud, and Jasper's every machination is designed to secure Rosa for himself.

At the point where the book breaks off, two principal questions are left unanswered. Has Edwin been murdered, or merely disappeared? And who is Datchery, the obviously disguised figure who has arrived in Cloisterham with the clear intention of exposing Jasper's game? It may be that Dickens intended Datchery as his detective, or that an official detective would have made his appearance later in the book had the author survived. The death of Charles Dickens, however, had the effect of creating one of the most famous literary puzzles of all time. It is still available today, in its incomplete form, published by Dent (Everyman's Library), OUP (Clarendon Dickens and New Oxford Illustrated Dickens) and Penguin.

With Dickens may be linked the name of Wilkie Collins (1824–1889), who today is not held in the esteem reserved for his illustrious contemporary but who nonetheless produced some exceptionally fine work. His well-known novel

COLLINS W Wilkie
The woman in white
Three volumes
Sampson Low 1860

is really a thriller rather than a detective novel, but still contains some of the features which later writers were to elaborate upon in the more intellectual field of the pure detective story. Its success was absolute, and its title – probably inspired by the lighthouse at Broadstairs in Kent – was quickly adopted by the worlds of fashion and cosmetics, providing ample proof that the cult figure is not purely a twentieth century phenomenon. The woman in the novel is mentally retarded and strongly resembles her half sister, who is an heiress. Duplicity, the starting point for so many great stories, develops into a complicated plot with such notable characterisation that Collins was for some time favourably compared with Dickens. Count Fosco is one of the few fat Italian villains of the time, whereas normally villains of melodrama were lean and hungry. The other character innovation has scarcely ever been repeated so memorably, that of introducing a heroine who is distinctly ugly. Many critics regard it as the finest sensational novel in English, and the reason is simply that Collins' command of the language was equal to his plotting ability.

The magnificent contribution which Wilkie Collins made to the history of detective fiction is encapsulated in his later novel

COLLINS W Wilkie
The moonstone. A romance
Three volumes
Tinsley Brothers 1868

which T S Eliot once described as 'the first, the longest and the best of English detective novels.' One may pedantically query each individual facet of this definition, without in any way detracting from the quality of this masterly work. It contains so many of the elements which subsequent writers were to use – the disappearance of a diamond, murder and suicide, opium, and so on. The story is narrated by each character in turn, in some cases by the use of letters and journals, and again this technique was to be used by later writers. To solve the mystery of the moonstone's disappearance is the task of Sergeant Cuff. He is 'grizzled . . . elderly . . . face as sharp as a hatchet.' Cuff, with his passion for roses and his throwaway lines of a type used later by Mason's Hanaud, is a brilliant portrait. His working methods, and much of the author's inspiration, were drawn from Inspector Whicher and the real life Constance Kent case of 1860.

The moonstone is currently available in Everyman's Library (Dent), World's Classics (OUP) and Penguin.

Although the contributions of Dickens and Collins were significant, it was stated earlier that the development of detective fiction was seen equally clear in France. In fact if anything the French contribution was even more clearly on the lines of the classic type of intellectual puzzle, and by far the most accomplished practitioner was Emile Gaboriau (1835-1873).

During his short life Gaboriau produced a comparatively large number of 'sensational' novels, and he is best remembered for his creation of a reasoning phenomenon who anticipated Sherlock Holmes by two decades. His name was Lecoq and he first appears in *L'affaire Lerouge* (1866) which in English translation became

GABORIAU Emile
The Lerouge case
Vizetelly 1885

but in this early case he is a pupil of Père Tabaret, formerly a pawnbroker's clerk and known as 'Tirauclaire'. Tabaret, an enthusiastic amateur, runs rings round the celebrated Gévrol of the Sûreté. He particularly excels in his astonishing knack of making all manner of deductions after the briefest examination of the scene of a crime, a knack which is communicated to young Lecoq and which the latter himself demonstrates in subsequent novels.

Tabaret inspects the scene of Widow Lerouge's murder, and immediately describes the assassin as 'a young man, a little above the middle height, elegantly dressed. He wore on that evening a high hat. He carried an umbrella, and smoked a trabucos with a cigar-holder.' Then, unlike some of fiction's most illustrious sleuths, he gives a full explanation of what led him to these conclusions. The tremendous popularity of Gaboriau's novels, with a readership which reputedly included Bismarck, inspired many imitators whose names were quickly forgotten. Some, however, built and improved upon Emile Gaboriau's techniques to establish even greater reputations for themselves. But to Gaboriau must go the credit for giving real impetus to the *roman policier* and the principles of deductive reasoning.

Lecoq takes the principal role, as its title implies, in *Monsieur Lecoq* (1869), published in Britain as

GABORIAU Emile
Lecoq, the detective
Two volumes
Vizetelly 1884

It is generally accepted that Monsieur Lecoq was inspired directly by Auguste Dupin, the detective created by Edgar Allan Poe, and that he also had a dash of Vidocq of the Sûreté. Nevertheless his use of logical deduction was something quite revolutionary in detective fiction, and he preceded Sherlock Holmes in his ability to construct a mental picture of a criminal by the examination of a few small clues which lesser mortals would fail even to notice.

There is little to choose between the various novels featuring Lecoq. All display his fantastic powers which captured the imagination of the public on both sides of the Channel until he was overshadowed in Britain by Sherlock Holmes. The critics' choice is probably *Le crime d'Orcival* (1867), which appeared in translation as

GABORIAU Emile
The mystery of Orcival
Vizetelly 1884

and begins with the discovery of a woman's body by two poachers. They are trespassing on the estate of the Count de Trémorel, and it soon appears that the count's chateau holds the key to the mystery. A man is accused of the murder – wrongly, thinks Lecoq – and the count himself has disappeared. Lecoq, sucking his inexhaustible supply of lozenges, propounds a solution and explains exactly how each clue provides a piece of the jigsaw, very much setting the pattern for hundreds of detective novelists yet to come.

Two more important books published between the ages of Poe and of Conan Doyle warrant mention here. Strangely enough, one was by a New Zealand author and set in Australia, whereas the other was American.

Among the many works of Fergus Hume (1859-1932) must be singled out

HUME Fergus W
Melbourne Kemp and Boyce 1886; Hansom Cab Publishing
   Company 1887

It seems incredible that this is probably the biggest bestseller in the history of detective fiction, as today it is scarcely remembered. The author too is a name which will be unfamiliar to many modern readers, in spite of the fact that he wrote well over a hundred books. Although its literary style is less attractive than many works of the period, it is in many ways representative of early detective fiction, and its phenomenal success must give it a place in a list of detective cornerstones. Its starting point is unusual – a man is found in a hansom cab in Melbourne, dead of chloroform poisoning. Samuel Gorby, detective of Melbourne City Police, investigates. One of the reasons for the book's popularity in Britain is almost certainly its overseas setting, and its portrayal of Melbourne life high and low. We see the city's leisured classes, but the detective must also follow trails through the Chinese slum quarters. The latter is a clear indication that Gaboriau influenced Hume.

Finally, the silence in the United States which surprisingly followed the master works of Edgar Allan Poe was finally broken – and uniquely so, for it saw the entry of a woman into the field. Anna Katharine Green (1846–1935) produced one work of particular distinction among her various detective novels, namely
   GREEN Anna Katharine
   The Leavenworth case, a lawyer's story
   New York Putnam 1878; A Strahan 1884
In spite of some stilted writing, it is an extremely important work. Ebenezer Gryce is a credible character of the period, 'a portly, comfortable personage.' We also see many of the features which were to become almost standard practice as new writers emerged – the body in the library, a diagram of the murder scene, and so on. It set the tone for a multitude of successors, and is by no means unenjoyable in its own right.

So by this time the stage was set for the emergence of a truly great detective, a major figure whose name was to become synonymous with the genre itself. And then, contrasting the very erratic development since the initiative taken by Poe, the floodgates were to open.

3 The great detective

It would be superfluous indeed to describe here in detail the Sherlock Holmes stories of Arthur Conan Doyle (1859–1930). Their background and history has been more than adequately covered elsewhere. The incredible mental faculties of Holmes, his life style and idiosyncrasies, and his exploits accompanied by friend and chronicler Dr John H Watson are already known to thousands of readers. Successive generations since 1887 have followed his adventures, and it would be no exaggeration to state that 221B Baker Street is to the foreign visitor as familiar an address as 10 Downing Street.

Furthermore the enquiring reader may be referred to Conan Doyle himself, who in *Memories and adventures* (Hodder & Stoughton 1924) not only acknowledges his debt to Gaboriau and Poe but describes how he modelled Holmes upon Dr Joseph Bell of Edinburgh.

Here therefore the emphasis will be bibliographical, and the earliest significant reference is the first appearance of Holmes in *A study in scarlet*, in *Beeton's christmas annual* for 1887. The first edition in book form followed soon afterwards. The success of

DOYLE A Conan
A study in scarlet
Ward, Lock 1888

resulted, strangely enough, in an American publication launching the next Holmes novel. *Lippincott's magazine,* in February 1890, began publication of *The sign of the four* but there was little delay before it was made available to British readers in volume form. The second definite article was eliminated from the title and since publication of

DOYLE A Conan
The sign of four
Spencer Blackett 1890

the title has remained in its latter form.

By this time Holmes had captured the public imagination, and George Newnes of the new *Strand magazine* made what transpired as a very shrewd move in securing Conan Doyle's services. Doyle was commissioned to write a series of Sherlock Holmes short stories, the first of which appeared in the *Strand* of July 1891. Further stories followed, and Holmes can be truly said to have come into his own. Most devotees consider that the short stories are infinitely preferable to the novels, as the particular skills of Holmes are better suited to the format; although Holmes can be a man of action when the situation demands, his gifts are primarily cerebral and his activities in the novels are supplemented by incidents, changes of scene and flashbacks which sometimes amount to little more than padding.

Following publication in the *Strand*, the first collection of short stories appeared as

DOYLE A Conan
The adventures of Sherlock Holmes
George Newnes 1892

The public clamoured for more, and in December 1892 the *Strand* began a new series of adventures which in turn were collectively published as

DOYLE A Conan
The memoirs of Sherlock Holmes
George Newnes 1894

but the last story in this series, *The final problem*, came to be regarded as almost a national disaster. 'It is with a heavy heart,' writes Dr Watson, 'that I take up my pen to write these last words in which I shall ever record the singular gifts by which my friend Mr Sherlock Holmes was distinguished.' The story concludes with the struggle above the Reichenbach Falls between Holmes and his arch enemy Moriarty, when both men plunge to their death. The country – indeed the world – was stunned.

The return of Holmes was vociferously demanded, but Conan Doyle had tired of him and was unyielding. He resolved to concentrate on other literature, but by 1901 public opinion began to have its effect and August of that year saw the serialisation in the *Strand* of *The hound of the Baskervilles*.

DOYLE A Conan
The hound of the Baskervilles. Another adventure of Sherlock Holmes
George Newnes 1902

was, however, only a small concession to the national appetite, for its text clearly stamps it as a posthumous adventure of Holmes. It is generally regarded as the best, and is certainly the most familiar, of the novels. This fresh exploit of the great detective led to renewed demands for more, and Conan Doyle capitulated in October 1903 with the first in a new series of *Strand* short stories. Collected as

> DOYLE A Conan
> The return of Sherlock Holmes
> George Newnes 1905

they begin with the resurrection of Holmes by a neat piece of author's licence and the volume contains stories which, even if they lack the standard of the earliest stories, still show much of the old flair.

Holmes' next appearance was in the novel *The valley of fear*, serialised in the *Strand* during 1914–1915 and published in volume form soon afterwards.

> DOYLE A Conan
> The valley of fear
> Smith, Elder 1915

has perhaps been somewhat less successful than the other Holmes adventures. At least it did not represent a rather dull end to a sparkling career, because it was followed by two more volumes of short stories. Following magazine publication, the final Holmes stories appeared as

> DOYLE A Conan
> His last bow: some reminiscences of Sherlock Holmes
> John Murray 1917

and

> DOYLE A Conan
> The case-book of Sherlock Holmes
> John Murray 1927

To remark that Sherlock Holmes has retained his popularity for almost ninety years would be an understatement. Indeed he is a national institution. The accolade is reflected in the fact that every Holmes adventure is still in print, and no discriminating reader of detective fiction can afford to be without

> DOYLE A Conan
> Sherlock Holmes: complete short stories
> John Murray 1928

which contains all fifty six of these perfect examples of the storyteller's art. This volume, together with

> DOYLE A Conan
> Sherlock Holmes: complete long stories
> John Murray 1928

comprises the entire Holmes canon.

Such was the impact of Holmes, and of course the lucrative nature of the stories, that he was bound to inspire countless imitators. Not only did other authors follow Conan Doyle's lead and create 'great detectives' of their own, but some added spice to the movement by giving their creations unique characteristics which set them apart from the Holmes band wagon.

They may be described as the 'rivals' of Sherlock Holmes, and it is regrettable that so many of them remained in the shadow of the master and are now long forgotten. Hugh Greene coined the phrase as the title of his anthology *The rivals of Sherlock Holmes* (The Bodley Head 1970; Penguin 1971), and performed a great service by bringing some of these gems of the past to the attention of today's readers. Such was the response, and the popularity of the television series thus inspired, that *More rivals of Sherlock Holmes* (The Bodley Head 1971; Penguin 1973) and *Crooked counties* (The Bodley Head 1973) followed.   .

One of the most accomplished contemporaries of Conan Doyle was Arthur Morrison (1863–1945), who is best known today for his

MORRISON Arthur
Martin Hewitt, investigator
Ward & Lock 1894

in addition to his stories of London low life such as *Tales of mean streets* and *The hole in the wall*. In Martin Hewitt he created a noteworthy rival of Sherlock Holmes, and the first volume was followed by

MORRISON Arthur
The chronicles of Martin Hewitt
Ward, Lock 1895

and

MORRISON Arthur
The adventures of Martin Hewitt
Ward, Lock 1896

Many writers of the period deliberately set out to make their detectives as unlike Holmes as possible, and Hewitt is in many respects a commonplace chap whose idiosyncrasies do not – as sometimes happens with Holmes – obtrude upon the stories.

Hewitt, like Holmes, made his first appearance in the *Strand magazine*, and has the occasional flash of intellectual brilliance equalling that of his illustrious contemporary. All in all, however, we see Hewitt as considerably less than omniscient, and are thus able to devote more attention to Morrison's ingenious plots, his characteristic London atmosphere, and his glimpses of many aspects of Victorian life.

Conan Doyle's brother in law, E W Hornung (1866–1921), created a memorable character in

HORNUNG E W

The amateur cracksman

Methuen 1899

which in later editions appeared as *Raffles, the amateur cracksman* (now Chatto). A J Raffles was not the first gentleman crook in fiction, but together with his contemporary Arsène Lupin he remains the best known. It was unusual for British readers of the time to identify and sympathise with a central character who makes his living by means of burglary, but Raffles has his redeeming features – his sense of fair play, his mastery of the game of cricket both literally and metaphorically. Then of course there is Bunny, his old school fag, who takes the part of the reader on occasions and attempts to persuade Raffles to return to the straight and narrow path. Unfortunately in the process Bunny finds himself more deeply involved in his master's burglarious activities.

Raffles is a romantic character, combining the high life of fashionable London society with the thrill of the chase brought about by his less sociable pursuits. In some of the stories he assumes the detective role, but normally it is as the anti-detective that he appears. The stories show him as a rogue rather than a complete villain. His love of country shines through the stories, and his further adventures in

HORNUNG E W

A thief in the night

Chatto & Windus 1905

culminate in his heroic death in the Boer War.

Raffles was not the only roguish hero of the time. There was more than a little dishonesty in the makeup of Romney Pringle, whose exploits were recorded by R Austin Freeman (1862–1943) at the outset of his literary career. Adopting the pseudonym 'Clifford Ashdown' he produced

ASHDOWN Clifford

The adventures of Romney Pringle

Ward, Lock 1902

with the collaboration of J J Pitcairn, a prison doctor. These short stories originally appeared in *Cassell's magazine* during 1902, as did a second series in 1903 which has never been published in book form. Indeed it is likely that any reader interested in the Romney Pringle stories will whet his appetite only if he has access to the original magazines or to anthologies in which individual stories have appeared. The

1902 volume is reputed to be the rarest book of detective short stories.

Mr Pringle is ostensibly a literary agent, and is a clean cut character 'whose complexion . . . was of that fairness which imparts to its fortunate possessor the air of youth until long past forty; especially in a man who shaves clean, and habitually goes to bed before two in the morning.' In other words, he is in direct contrast with the drugtaking insomniac Holmes. Although like Holmes he is a master of disguise, he differs again from the sage of Baker Street in that he is no professional detective. Rather is he someone with an unfortunate knack of getting involved in other people's misfortunes, and he frequently turns them to his own pecuniary advantage. Pringle is a likeable rogue who lives by his wits and lines his pocket at the expense of the real villains.

Freeman later dropped the Ashdown pseudonym, and was in fact not happy with his Romney Pringle stories. Using his own name he wrote

FREEMAN R Austin
The red thumb mark
Collingwood 1907

and introduced his most celebrated character, Dr John Thorndyke. A detective novel without a murder is a comparatively rare phenomenon, but several examples have found places as cornerstones in the history of the genre. This is one of them, and the absence of a corpse makes it no less enthralling. Diamonds are stolen from a safe, and a thumb print in blood is found nearby. Moreover the thumb print is identified and a man is charged. But Dr Thorndyke, probably the most famous medico scientific detective in fiction, thrives on lost causes. Such an open-and-shut case, with the new technique of fingerprinting on the side of the prosecution, is just the sort of challenge Thorndyke relishes. He is assisted as usual by Polton and Jervis, and survives several ingenious attempts on his life which convince him that he is on the right track. There is, however, one major question which remains unanswered until the final stages of the trial – is it possible to forge a thumb print?

The creator of the Scarlet Pimpernel, Baroness Orczy (1865–1947), also produced some very acceptable detective fiction, and in

ORCZY Baroness
The case of Miss Elliott . . . Illustrated
T Fisher Unwin 1905

she presented a character who, physically at least, derived nothing

29

whatsoever from Sherlock Holmes. The old man in the corner is bird-like, with watery eyes, spectacles, and bony fingers tying knots in pieces of string. He is always to be found in his seat in the ABC tea shop. Thus he is one of the first 'armchair detectives' of fiction, in that he solves his cases by pure process of thought and scarcely ever moves from his seat. The stories are narrated by a young journalist, Polly Burton, who sits entranced as her acquaintance sifts the newspapers for crimes and arrives at their solutions in little more than the time it takes to consume his inevitable cheesecake. The stories are skilfully contrived, eminently readable, and contain little extraneous matter.

The case of Miss Elliott was the first volume of Old Man stories to be published, although some had appeared earlier in *The royal magazine* and were collected subsequently as

> ORCZY Baroness
> The old man in the corner . . . Illustrated by H M Brock
> Greening 1909

Another original detective created by Baroness Orczy is Patrick Mulligan. 'Fat and rosy and comfortable as an Irish pig', Mulligan is a lawyer who in

> ORCZY Baroness
> 'Skin o' my tooth' His memoirs, by his confidential clerk
> Hodder & Stoughton 1928

uses his exceptional gifts of acumen and intuition to extricate his clients from the various messes into which they have tumbled. His sobriquet is believed by his clerk, Mullins, to have been devised by one such client who was acquitted by the skin of his teeth, and in this volume Mullins narrates twelve of his chief's celebrated cases. Although not a well known book today, the stories are neatly plotted and enjoyable.

Robert Barr (1850–1912) was a prolific writer whose best work in the detective field was

> BARR Robert
> The triumphs of Eugène Valmont
> Hurst & Blackett 1906

It has been suggested that Valmont, a French detective operating in London, was the model for Agatha Christie's Belgian maestro Her-cule Poirot, and whether or not this is true they are decidedly of a type. Valmont is depicted as vain, pompous, and of course comic, and the official policeman as personified by Spenser Hale is a fallible being, qualified to be no more than Valmont's confidant. It may be that Barr was merely setting out to be humorous, but equally he might have deliberately intended to satirise Anglo-French difficulties. Even if deep study of these stories is less than profitable, they provide sound plots of considerable ingenuity. Some of them, particularly *The absent minded coterie*, are *tours de force* which have found places in detective anthologies, and the whole volume warrants reprinting for the benefit of modern readers.

Among the victims of the *Titanic* disaster was a man of thirty seven named Jacques Futrelle (1875–1912), an American whose life was cut short at a time when he was regarded as one of detective fiction's white hopes. His fame was founded, and remains firmly based, upon his sheer ingenuity and his creation of one of the most original characters in the field. Professor Augustus S F X Van Dusen first appeared in

FUTRELLE Jacques
The thinking machine . . . illustrated by the Kinneys
New York Dodd, Mead 1907; Chapman & Hall 1907

These stories demonstrate, as the title sobriquet infers, the tremendous brain power of this man whose academic brilliance – he has degrees from half the world's universities – is matched by an enviable intellect. Logic, he insists, will solve any problem. In *The problem of cell 13* he wagers that he will escape from a closely guarded prison merely by using his mind, and in subsequent stories he cuts through the evidence in various criminal cases by the application of sheer logic.

FUTRELLE Jacques
The thinking machine on the case
New York D Appleton 1908

was the second volume, called *The professor on the case* for the British edition, published as Nelson's library no 62 (Nelson 1909). In it we are reminded of how he received his nickname. He defeats a Russian chess master after merely learning the rudiments of the game. '"You are a brain – a machine – a thinking machine",' says the Russian. The Professor's grotesque appearance, with his enormous head invariably wearing a 'number eight hat', makes him a memorable character physically, but the brain is the main thing in these stories. He is faced with some of the most unusual cases to be devised by any author. One can instance *The superfluous finger*, which opens when an eminent surgeon is visited by a beautiful woman. '"The forefinger,"' she explains calmly. '"I should like to have it amputated at the first joint, please."' And so another mystery occupies the Professor's mind. Were it not for Futrelle's untimely death he would probably have improved even upon these nearly perfect stories.

The rivals of Sherlock Holmes were created predominantly by British writers, but the Gallic equivalent of Hornung's Raffles was the brainchild of Maurice Leblanc (1864–1941). In the volume of stories called

> LEBLANC Maurice
> The seven of hearts, together with other exploits of Arsène Lupin . . . Translated by A. Teixeira de Mattos. With illustrations by Cyrus Cuneo
> Cassell 1908

and subsequently retitled *The exploits of Arsène Lupin* (Cassell 1909), the hero is shown in roughly the same light as Raffles. He is a thief, but basically a decent enough chap. He also champions the underdog and ladies in distress, and spends a considerable amount of time running rings around the English detective Holmlock Shears (note the family likeness). Although in the later books Lupin often assumes the role of amateur detective, it is in the earlier stories as the gentleman burglar, the master of disguise, that he is at his most entertaining. To enlist the reader's sympathy and association, he bites the biter or exercises his villainy on the more obnoxious members of society, providing an enduring form of sheer escapism.

A compatriot and contemporary of Maurice Leblanc, although writing in a different vein, Gaston Leroux (1868–1927) was a journalist whose occupation enabled him to acquire considerable experience of courtroom procedure. He made excellent use of this, and the drama generated during a murder trial, in the one detective novel for which he is remembered

> LEROUX Gaston
> The mystery of the yellow room . . . Illustrated by Cyrus Cuneo
> ('Daily Mail' Sixpenny Novels No 54)
> Daily Mail 1908

contained devices which have been used by scores of subsequent writers, namely the 'locked room' murder and the 'least likely person' exposed in the final pages. Most authorities claim that Leroux was greatly influenced by an earlier novel, *The big bow mystery* by Israel Zangwill (Henry 1891), although the deductive element in which the reader can participate is much more evident in Leroux's work. As a locked room puzzle it was admired by John Dickson Carr – praise indeed, considering Carr's absolute mastery of this particular technique.

The detective Joseph Rouletabille is a young and precocious journalist whose name has been assured of a place in the annals of crime fiction by his performance in this one case. In contrast with many books of the period it is highly readable even today, if one overlooks the emphasis on coincidence and the many examples of improbability. Neither of these traits can be ruled totally out of court in the classic, as opposed to the realistic, detective novel.

One can not get further from Sherlock Holmes than Father Brown, the classic character created by G K Chesterton (1874–1936). He made his first appearance in

> CHESTERTON G K
> The innocence of Father Brown . . . with eight full-page plates
>   by Sydney Seymour Lucas
> Cassell 1911

and is still very much with us today, the little priest from Essex with 'face as round as a Norfolk dumpling' and 'eyes as empty as the North Sea'. He has reached an even wider audience through the medium of television, which has succeeded in showing the sheer cleverness of these masterpieces of detection. The stories must be read, however, to appreciate Chesterton's brilliant use of words, his characterisation, and his thesis that the commonplace can be startling because it is so often overlooked. For examples of the latter, see *The invisible man* and *The queer feet* – both deservedly classics of the genre. If some of the stories are sermons, they are still the most enjoyable sermons ever delivered.

Following his initial success Father Brown reappeared in *The wisdom of Father Brown* (Cassell 1914; now Penguin), *The incredulity of Father Brown* (Cassell 1926; now Penguin), *The secret of Father Brown* (Cassell 1927) and *The scandal of Father Brown* (Cassell 1935). The first four volumes were collected together in

> CHESTERTON G K
> The Father Brown stories
> Cassell 1929

which is an essential item in any collection.

All too often writers have descended to sheer gimmickry in order to make their detective characters stand out from the others. Ernest Bramah (1868–1942), however, had a brilliant idea rather than a gimmick. The detective in

> BRAMAH Ernest

33

Max Carrados
Methuen 1914

is blind, but his blindness has heightened his other senses, and thus it is an integral factor in the stories which Bramah contrived. This puts the detective on a somewhat different level to the reader and perhaps is a little less than fair, but the stories are nonetheless enjoyable. The three volumes of Carrados cases, in which he is accompanied by an unusually sensible assistant called Louis Carlyle, comprise a mixture of cases from robbery to murder, kidnapping to sabotage. All the stories are worth reading, being competently written with a lightness of touch as well as meticulously plotted. The two subsequent volumes

BRAMAH Ernest
The eyes of Max Carrados
Grant Richards 1923

and

BRAMAH Ernest
Max Carrados mysteries
Hodder & Stoughton 1927

each contain examples of the sort of thing which has placed Ernest Bramah among the greats of detective fiction.

The history of detective fiction is bestrewn with the names of authors who, once popular, are now completely forgotten. Many of them deserved this fate, and a rereading of their work today will serve only to make their original popularity seem quite unjustified. There are mixed opinions regarding Arthur B Reeve (1880–1936), who sprang to fame with his tales of Craig Kennedy and particularly

REEVE Arthur B
The silent bullet: the adventures of Craig Kennedy, scientific
    detective
New York Dodd, Mead 1912; Hodder & Stoughton 1916

His large following is undeniable, and some may find it incredible. It was assisted by his activities in the field of silent movies, where he wrote melodramatic serials with titles such as *The exploits of Elaine*. His name must appear in any representative list of detective fiction, however, as the creator of one of the earliest scientific detectives. White coated Kennedy alternates between the laboratory and the field of battle in a series of adventures which reflect Reeve's passable narrative ability and a whole succession of ingenious scientific devices. Many of the latter were novel in their day, but soon became either commonplace or else discredited figments of the writer's imagination.

Perhaps this is the principal reason why Reeve, at one time the foremost American writer of crime fiction, sank later into oblivion.

And finally, although he did not appear until 1918, one must not fail to include Uncle Abner as a rival of Sherlock Holmes. One of the few American exponents at this time, Melville Davisson Post (1871–1930) made his supreme contribution with

POST Melville Davisson
Uncle Abner, master of mysteries
New York and London D Appleton 1918

There is something of the Old Testament prophet in Uncle Abner, the West Virginia squire whose exposure of evildoers is recounted in stories which have been described as the best since Poe. These tales appeared in magazines before publication in book form, and were roughly contemporaneous with Chesterton's Father Brown. Uncle Abner, accompanied by his nephew and Squire Randolph, encounter evil in many forms. Abner has the capacity to see it in men's souls, and woe betide them.

But these are not just stories of a ranting, hellfire and damnation character. The points are often small which bring a murderer to justice or to meet his maker, but they are devilishly ingenious in the hands of Uncle Abner. The fertile imagination of Melville Davisson Post, together with his absolute mastery of the short story format, combine to make Abner unforgettable.

4   The traditional twenties

The development of detective fiction tends to be categorised by its historians into neatly defined periods. Howard Haycraft in the excellent *Murder for pleasure* has described the period from Sherlock Holmes to the outbreak of the first world war as 'The Romantic Era', and 1918 to 1930 as 'The Golden Age'. Everything following that, to Haycraft writing in 1941, was of course modern. Julian Symons in *Bloody murder* thirty years after Haycraft, could naturally see things in perspective and identifies the rivals of Sherlock Holmes as appearing in the 'First Golden Age' and a 'Second Golden Age' embracing the twenties and thirties. Various authors began to break away from the traditional pattern in the thirties, both in terms of form (Francis Iles *et al*) and in terms of content (Hammett and the hardboiled school). They are still, in Julian Symons' treatment of the subject, within the 'Second Golden Age', and the moderns date from the second world war.

No-one has denied, however, that considerable overlaps occurred between these various eras. In the golden thirties – golden at least as far as crime fiction was concerned – there were omniscient sleuths of the Holmes variety in addition to authors who in style were years ahead of their time. Even today, when the cosy detective story has been so nearly smothered by a superfluity of sex and violence, there are new writers of the classic school emerging. One thing is certain. In the confused history of crime fiction, the twenties were almost completely traditional.

Edgar Wallace (1875–1932) was very much a writer of the twenties, although his first crime novel appeared as early as 1905. When first published

> WALLACE Edgar
> The four just men
> Tallis Press 1905

was incomplete. The final chapter, in which the solution to the 'locked room' murder mystery is explained, only appears in subsequent editions of the book. The first edition contains a tearout form offering £500 in prizes to the most accurate solutions furnished by readers. A clever idea, but Wallace was on the losing end financially as it turned out. The four just men, as by now is well known, are idealists who murder in cases where the law is unable to act, and where despots and tyrants would otherwise go free. Thus they have the reader's sympathy from the beginning. This, the incredible Edgar Wallace's debut in the field in which he was to become a phenomenon, culminates in the seemingly impossible murder of the Foreign Secretary behind closed doors, with half the Metropolitan Police keeping watch. Anyone fortunate enough to possess a copy of the first edition will, of course, have to devise his own ending or consult the later edition (Newnes 1911).

What was the secret of Wallace's popularity? Perhaps one of his best known works

WALLACE Edgar
The Crimson Circle
Hodder & Stoughton 1922

provides the answer. He was a craftsman storyteller, completely without literary pretensions, an easy read untaxing of the intellect. Many of his books followed set patterns, and were thrillers rather than detective stories. There is, however, rather more of the detective element in this case, where we follow the police on the track of master criminal and multiple murderer The Crimson Circle. His subordinates obey him without question, or die. His victims pay with their money or their lives. He seems unassailable – but Inspector Parr and the psychometric Derrick Yale know his identity, and all is revealed in the final few pages.

So many detectives and heroic characters dash through the pages of Wallace's work – most of them faceless and wooden – that his memorable Mr Reeder comes as a welcome surprise. In

WALLACE Edgar
The mind of Mr J G Reeder
Hodder & Stoughton 1925

we are introduced to this unassuming man who works for the Public Prosecutor. He is a gem of a character, Victorian in appearance and manners, with his sidewhiskers and pince-nez and his umbrella which is never unfurled. He also has his catchphrase, '"I have a criminal mind"', and the stories demonstrate his skill at recognising evil when it is at hand. One can go so far as to state that this collection of eight stories, polished and neatly plotted, represents Wallace's supreme contribution to the field of detection as opposed to action thrillers.

Another writer popular during the twenties, who like Wallace began much earlier, was Mary Roberts Rinehart (1876–1958). Her books in fact spanned several decades. In

RINEHART Mary Roberts
The circular staircase . . . With illustrations by Lester Ralph
Indianapolis Bobbs-Merrill 1908; Cassell 1909

a middle aged spinster rents a furnished house for the summer, something of a mansion with an eerie atmosphere aggravated by a rather mysterious circular staircase. It is not long before our heroine is plagued by uninvited nocturnal visitors, one of whom is murdered. From this point on, the spinster narrator plunges headlong into the adventure in true Rinehart tradition. This was her first book, and retains a quality of eminent readability. It also demonstrates her faults, such as the excessive use of coincidence and the withholding of important clues from the official detective.

'Had I but known how important this was, four lives would have been saved,' is the sort of statement which occurs frequently in her works and those of her imitators. In fact it has been described as the 'Had I But Known' school. But in spite of the scorn of the critics, there is no pretentiousness about Mary Roberts Rinehart and her melodramas, and one must admit she tells a good story, meticulously plotted, and moreover it is all great fun.

A work which is as familiar today as in the twenties is

BENTLEY E C
Trent's last case
Nelson 1913

Strangely enough, Bentley wrote no detective fiction in the twenties, and this particular novel was originally intended, as its title implies, to be the only appearance of Philip Trent. Bentley revived Trent during the 1930s but with little of the skill shown in the original.

The murder of tycoon Sigsbee Manderson is the sort of event which provides ample newspaper copy, although it is soon obvious that not everyone mourns his passing. Bentley deliberately set out to write a detective novel with a difference, breaking with tradition in several respects; almost a revelation of some of the genre's weaknesses. His use of humour, his love interest, and to cap it all the detective proving all too fallible, are all contrary to the canons of detective fiction accepted at the time the book was written. And Philip Trent, artist and journalist, is less than a great detective in the Holmes tradition.

Possibly to the author's surprise he had written what turned out to be a bestseller.

E C Bentley's master work was very much in the flavour of the twenties although written earlier, and the same can be said of the novels of A E W Mason (1865–1948). His famous book

MASON A E W
At the Villa Rose
Hodder & Stoughton 1910

concerns the murder of a wealthy widow at Aix-les-Bains, and introduces one of the indisputably great fictional detectives, Inspector Hanaud of the Paris Sûreté. Like Holmes he has his Watson – the elderly Mr Ricardo, whose knowledge of food and wine is matched only by his inability to fathom the various clues as he follows the detective around. It is a period piece, and displays the classic form as Hanaud skilfully picks his way through pieces of evidence and false trails. One of his more irritating habits is his failure to explain the significance of the clues as he finds them, so we are left in the dark until he finally springs the solution upon us. After the revelation of the murderer's identity there are several chapters of flashback showing how the crime was planned and committed, which modern readers might find somewhat flat.

The second Hanaud novel

MASON A E W
The house of the arrow
Hodder & Stoughton 1924

was published fourteen years after the first, and many critics have judged it to be better. It shows Mason to be a serious novelist who is interested in communicating the fine gradations of the human character more than merely presenting a puzzle and its solution. Solicitor Jim Frobisher receives a letter from a rich woman's brother in law demanding an advance on her will. The woman dies and her niece is arrested. Back to the south, to Dijon this time, hurries Inspector Hanaud to investigate the mystery. The big man is likened to a St Bernard dog, but nevertheless is one of the sharpest policemen in fiction and his cases are always triumphs of deductive reasoning.

The world of crime fiction has produced several writers who, for various reasons, can be described as phenomena. One such is J S Fletcher (1863–1935), whose fame dates from

FLETCHER J S
The Middle Temple murder

Ward, Lock 1919

which was praised by President Woodrow Wilson, and established a vogue for Fletcher's books in the USA as well as in his native England. From the moment journalist Frank Spargo is involved in the discovery of a body in Middle Temple Lane, the pace is faster than many detective novels of the period and the atmosphere of London is well conveyed. Although he skilfully depicted the English country scene with a love of the open spaces befitting a Yorkshireman, it is for Fletcher's London novels that he is remembered, another of them being

FLETCHER J S
The Charing Cross mystery
Herbert Jenkins 1923

When Hetherwick, a young barrister, catches the last train at Sloane Square he is unaware that within a few minutes he will be playing detective. At St James's Park two men board the train, and by the time it reaches Charing Cross one of them has died. It is a nicely contrived mystery with a dash of London authenticity, although modern commuters on the Circle and District lines are unlikely to experience an adventure quite so exciting – or fast moving! But to revert to our first point, why can Fletcher be described as a phenomenon? The reason is simply that he is virtually unknown today, and yet for a period he was one of the biggest names in the field on both sides of the Atlantic. He exercised a great influence on the popularisation of detective fiction, his main faults being his descent into melodrama on occasions and his frequently poor characterisation. Nevertheless he inspired others, who in turn were more accomplished, and for that he should be remembered.

Dr Reginald Fortune is another character who is not as familiar to present day readers as he perhaps ought to be. It is a strange verdict on the dozen or so books in which he appeared, and which made H C Bailey (1878–1961) one of the top crime writers of the twenties and thirties. Admittedly Fortune – plumply cherubic, facetious, drawling - can be intensely irritating at times, but nevertheless he brings to the stories a freshness and a nice intuitiveness that few of the great detectives can match. H C Bailey was at his best in the short story form, the first volume in the series being

BAILEY H C
Call Mr Fortune
Methuen 1920

which was followed by other collections of roughly comparable standard.

An important landmark in the history of detective fiction,

CROFTS Freeman Wills
The cask
Collins 1920

was the first work of an author who established a reputation for solid, plodding, logical detection and an almost fanatical attention to detail. Crofts (1879–1957) specialised in the unbreakable alibi, often based upon railway timetables. In his most famous book, the cask of the title is being unloaded after a voyage from Rouen to London. It should contain statuary; instead it contains sovereigns and a woman's hand. Not only that, but it disappears before the police arrive. The clues tell a story which alternates between France and England, and we follow two detectives – Inspector Burnley and George La Touche – on their painstaking paths through an unusually long story before the last piece of the puzzle fits into place.

The unsensational detective work typically displayed by Crofts might not be to every reader's liking. None of his plots can be described as racy or fast moving, but perhaps

CROFTS Freeman Wills
The pit-prop syndicate
Collins 1922

is one which combines the elements of the thriller and the detective novel rather well. The activities of the syndicate, ostensibly shipping pit props from France to England, are stumbled upon by two amateur detectives. Beyond suspecting that dirty work is afoot they know little else, but are determined to investigate. Murder follows, and the professional detective Inspector Willis takes over.

CROFTS Freeman Wills
Inspector French's greatest case
Collins 1925

marked the first appearance of the Scotland Yard man who was to become something of an institution. It opens with the discovery of a corpse near the rifled safe of a diamond merchant in Hatton Garden. French gets to work in a way which, for many years and many novels to follow, he was to make very much his own; meticulous, skilful, plodding, as neatly dovetailed as the railway timetables which so often were his stock in trade. Call them what you will, the French stories are undeniably the product of a brilliantly logical mind. One receives the impression that the work of a Scotland Yard man is singularly unexciting, and this somehow endows all the work of Freeman Wills Crofts with the stamp of authenticity. Pedantic and unexciting it may be, but the reader works side by side with French until the break comes and the loose ends are neatly tied up.

MILNE A A
The Red House mystery
Methuen 1922

may be described as typical of the period rather than outstandingly accomplished, although it has subsequently appeared in many editions. A A Milne (1882–1956) attempts to be conventional – the country house party, the murder of the black sheep of the family, the amateur detective and his rather silly confidant. The ultimate revelation of the murderer comes hardly as a surprise, although it has its clever touches. One can only define it as the 'here's a murder, what fun!' school and in a way wish that the author had stuck to Winnie the Pooh, but it is often quoted as a cornerstone of 1920s detective fiction.

Quick to follow in the footsteps of Freeman Wills Crofts was G D H Cole (1890–1959), renowned as a Fabian economist. As a diversion Cole turned to detective fiction and produced

COLE G D H
The Brooklyn murders
Collins 1923

The last will and testament of theatre impresario Sir Vernon Brooklyn is the starting point, and three deaths are clearly linked with the ultimate disposal of his fortune. The case is handled by Superintendent Wilson of Scotland Yard, who was to feature in many subsequent novels. Known as The Professor in allusion to his scholarly habits and his pre-eminently intellectualist way of reasoning out the solution to his cases, Wilson is an investigator of the Inspector French school. He does not appear, however, to get out of his room at the Yard to the same extent as most policemen in fiction; he prefers instead to let Inspector Blaikie do the leg work and much of the questioning of suspects, and Wilson himself sits and exercises his intellectual faculties upon all the reports which Blaikie provides. Following Wilson's debut, G D H Cole embarked upon a succession of detective novels in collaboration with his wife, and probably the best of these is

COLE G D H and Margaret
The murder at Crome House
Collins 1927

The criticism levelled at the Coles is that, particularly by modern standards, their novels are dull. It is true that many passages consist of routine interviews with suspects, and that Superintendent Wilson then thoroughly sifts all the evidence and proceeds systematically towards discrediting the guilty party's alibi. Nevertheless it must be appreciated that this type of detective fiction was a popular form in the twenties and thirties, and that the examples produced by the Coles – together of course with those of Crofts – were among the best of an extremely large bunch. They are well written, they hold the reader's interest most of the time, and the detective puzzles are on occasions ingenious. Although the later output of the Coles became somewhat slapdash the earlier stories are well worth reading.

The Crome House case is in fact a non-Wilson novel with rather more pace than their other works. Somewhat lightheartedly it follows the adventures of university lecturer James Flint, an amateur detective who becomes involved in the murder of Sir Harry Wye. Sir Harry, described as a first class old rip, follows tradition by being murdered in his library. The absence of a detective of the omniscient variety, and the complications of the plot, are factors which make this novel stand out from others by the Cole partnership.

Another writer of competence was Major Cecil Street (1884–1964), who under the pseudonym 'John Rhode' produced a succession of straightforward detective novels spanning three decades. His first was

RHODE John
The Paddington mystery
Geoffrey Bles 1925

and is listed here as purely representative of his long list of conventional tales. Rhode's principal character, Dr Priestley, is a mathematician who employs pure scientific analysis rather than any flair for the intuitional approach. The Priestley novels may be humdrum on occasions, but are dependable and solid. Few writers, if any, can claim to equal Rhode in the variations of ingenious murder methods he contrived over the years. Of his other works, perhaps the mass murder case

RHODE John
The murders in Praed Street
Geoffrey Bles 1928

can be singled out as one which deserves to survive.

Among the multitude of detective characters created in the twenties and thirties, some were sufficiently original for their names to be still remembered some fifty years later. Others, on the other hand, developed into something even more, a cult with timeless popularity which has been uniformly sustained. One such is Charlie Chan, the Chinese-Hawaiian yet distinctly American mixture whose principal adventures were collected in

BIGGERS Earl Derr
Celebrated cases of Charlie Chan
Indianapolis Bobbs-Merrill 1933; Cassell 1933

One of the main reasons for Charlie's success is probably that at the time of his conception it was customary for fictional Chinese to be the villains, and new ground was broken when Biggers (1884–1933) introduced a Chinese detective. Subsequently he was portrayed on radio and television, and in a host of motion pictures and comics. The original stories themselves, somewhat contrived and looking a little like period pieces today, will nevertheless remain significant. They represented an important era in American crime fiction and introduced us to the urbane Charlie and his mannerisms. The compendium volume, essential in any collection, comprises *The house without a key* (Bobbs-Merrill 1925; Harrap 1926); *The Chinese parrot* (Bobbs-Merrill 1926; Harrap 1927); *Behind that curtain* (Bobbs-Merrill 1928; Harrap 1928); *The black camel* (Bobbs-Merrill 1929; Cassell 1930); and *Charlie Chan carries on* (Bobbs-Merrill 1930; Cassell 1931).

VAN DINE S S
The Benson murder case
New York Scribner 1926; Ernest Benn 1926

was the first in a series of twelve novels featuring Philo Vance, one of the most famous amateur detectives of the 1920s. The author, alias art critic Willard Huntington Wright (1888–1939), set out to present problems in detection in which he followed a code of rules, every detail being carefully and scrupulously fitted into its place like a jigsaw. The Benson case concerns the murder of a wealthy New York stockbroker and *bon viveur*. The suspects are restricted in number, and Philo Vance smoothly proceeds to a very satisfactory solution. Vance himself, a dilettante with a penchant for intellectual oneupmanship and a pseudo English manner of speaking, is a somewhat irritating creation. Equally affected at times is the author's excessive use of footnotes to amplify the artistic or literary allusions to which Vance is so partial. Perhaps, however, these helped to give the novels their special flavour. In any case they quickly became the best known American detective fiction since Poe, and comparatively few writers have subsequently been placed in that category.

The second Philo Vance novel,

VAN DINE S S
The canary murder case
New York Scribner 1927; Ernest Benn 1927

fully established the author's reputation and broke publishing records in the field of detective fiction. The canary of the title is Margaret Odell, star of Broadway, who gained the name after appearing in a follies ballet in a canary costume. Her scintillating rise to fame is cut short suddenly when she is strangled, in circumstances which bring Philo Vance into the case. He is as usual accompanied by John F-X Markham, District Attorney of New York, who is not the brightest of confidants but nonetheless habitually gets the kudos for solving the Vance cases. This novel shows the Van Dine style and ingenuity beginning to develop, and is a good example of 1920s detection.

There is little to choose between one Van Dine novel and another, except that his last two or three were markedly inferior. Possibly the best are

VAN DINE S S
The Greene murder case
New York Scribner 1928; Ernest Benn 1928

in which Vance investigates a series of murders which occur in one ill-fated family, and

VAN DINE S S
The Bishop murder case
New York Scribner 1929; Cassell 1929

with its terrifying series of murders connected with the old nursery rhyme, *Who killed Cock Robin?*

45

An underrated writer of the period was C H B Kitchin (1896–1967), who wrote

> KITCHIN C H B
> Death of my aunt
> L & V Woolf 1929

Stockbroker Malcolm Warren is the obvious person to advise his monied aunt about her financial affairs, and he visits her for just that purpose. When she is poisoned, and it seems that the solution to the mystery is within the family circle, Malcolm finds himself playing the amateur detective. Although Kitchin was no innovator in the field, his books have a cosiness, a slightly lighthearted flavour, a thorough Englishness which critics have admired. What is more, his ideas were channelled into very few books, in contrast to many writers of the time who produced a flood of potboilers.

Urbane, witty, humorous, satirical; any one of these words can be used to describe the Roger Sheringham novels by Anthony Berkeley (1893–1971). In

> BERKELEY Anthony
> The poisoned chocolates case
> Collins 1929

we are presented with one in a unique form. The six members of the Crimes Circle are gathered together to consider the murder of Mrs Joan Bendix, as recounted by Chief Inspector Moresby of Scotland Yard. Then, one by one, they give their solutions to the mystery. To devise six solutions in one detective novel, and to demolish them just as quickly, requires a brilliant mind. A rereading of Anthony Berkeley today, especially this one, will convince anyone that the history of crime fiction owes him a debt as a masterly practitioner and an innovator.

Berkeley wrote also as 'Francis Iles', and displayed remarkable versatility ranging from pure detection to the forerunner of the modern crime novel. One of his most enjoyable works is

> BERKELEY Anthony
> Trial and error
> Hodder & Stoughton 1937

not the least for its delightful central character Mr Lawrence Todhunter. Mr Todhunter's doctor gives him only a few months to live, and he decides to occupy his time by planning and carrying out the murder of someone whose death would be a distinct gain to the world. He decides to shoot Jean Norwood, a celebrated and bitchy actress, as his final contribution to society. It is after the murder is committed that complications begin to arise, as another man is arrested and the police refuse to accept Mr Todhunter's confession. There must be very few detective novels in which the central character has to prove his own guilt. Assuming there are others, this must be the best – and the one with the most unpredictable ending.

Some of the writers flourishing in the twenties were still producing new work in the thirties and forties, or even later. But one, Agatha Christie, began in the year 1920 and has written at least one each year since then. Mrs Christie is featured in the next section with three other 'Queens of Crime'. Between them they were responsible for a truly phenomenal number of fine detective stories which spanned more than five decades.

5 Queens of crime

This section recognises the distinction of four writers by pinpointing their best works, segregating them from their contemporaries. No apology is made for this, as the four writers concerned have all created detective fiction of the very highest standard and they do not fit neatly into the period divisions of this bibliography.

The creator of Lord Peter Wimsey, Dorothy L Sayers (1893–1957) produced fewer books than the other three writers covered by this section. In addition to the shorter duration of her writing career, she also displayed less interest in the detective story *per se* and a developing trend towards the novel of manners. Her most unusual detective novel, indeed unusual by any standards, was

SAYERS Dorothy L and EUSTACE Robert
The documents in the case
Ernest Benn 1930

which is told entirely by means of documents. Letters, telegrams, statements and newspaper reports are reproduced in a most effective manner. It is still, perhaps surprisingly, an enthralling detective story. It is also a classic in the field of 'medical' mysteries, thanks presumably to joint author Robert Eustace, who collaborated with many authors over a lengthy period on plots involving forensic medicine.

The skill of Dorothy L Sayers was evident in her short stories as clearly as in her novels. Indeed the volumes of short stories could be decidedly more to the taste of some readers, as her novels have been criticised for the way in which the detective element sometimes takes second place to Lord Peter's family affairs. If there is extraneous material in her novels, it is not seen in the clever cases collected under the general title

SAYERS Dorothy L
Hangman's holiday
Victor Gollancz 1933

We also get a change from Lord Peter, as most of the stories feature the humorous Mr Montague Egg, wine salesman and amateur detective. Without Lord Peter a totally different Miss Sayers emerges. There are also two little masterpieces without a central detective, which in style may be compared with the work of Roy Vickers and Cyril Hare.

The investigations of Lord Peter Wimsey, however, are the basis of Dorothy L Sayers' reputation. Of these, special mention must be made of

SAYERS Dorothy L
The nine tailors
Victor Gollancz 1934

It is rare to find a detective novel with a specialised background where neither the detective puzzle nor the authenticity of the background suffers. This classic of death among the changeringers of an East Anglian village is just such a one. Its details of bellringing are clearly the result of patient research, and the activities of the villagers of Fenchurch St Paul are related with loving care. After all, it is the sort of East Anglian village with salt-of-the-earth characters who have been pursuing the same activities year in and year out, and where nothing untoward ever happens. That is, until the day a savagely mutilated corpse is found in the graveyard. Lord Peter finds that campanology is of greater assistance to him than criminology, but he fortunately has a smattering of both.

Most detective novels rely upon murder as the mainspring of the plot, possibly because readers until comparatively recently were inclined to feel the thrill of the chase more keenly in cases where the criminal was risking the supreme penalty. It was therefore something of a gamble on the part of Dorothy L Sayers when at the peak of her career she produced the bloodless

SAYERS Dorothy L
Gaudy night
Victor Gollancz 1935

but in fact it has become a classic. Harriet Vane, mystery novelist, returns to her old Oxford college and becomes involved in an unpleasant outbreak of poison pen letters. Although she sets out to investigate the affair herself, she soon enlists the aid of Lord Peter Wimsey, who previously secured Harriet's acquittal in the murder case entitled *Strong poison* (Victor Gollancz 1930).

The university setting is skilfully portrayed, and the detective puzzle succeeds admirably in spite of the absence of corpses, but some writers have criticised the author for deliberately attempting to transform the detective novel into something it was never intended to be. Certainly in this case there is much that is entertaining in the book and the detective element is by no means the be-all and end-all, but it was not until

> SAYERS Dorothy L
> Busman's honeymoon. A love story with detective inter-
> ruptions
> Victor Gollancz 1937

that she made her intention plain, as witness the subtitle. Lord Peter and Harriet decide to make it legal at last, and following a great deal of society chitchat they set off on their honeymoon. The house unfortunately has been conveyed to Lord Peter complete with a dead body, and this provides the detective interruptions which are in fact another clear demonstration of Miss Sayers' plotting ability.

Possibly her acknowledged skill as a detective novelist made her readers expect more and more of her, and inclined some to dislike the romanticising to which she was prone. It has even been suggested that she became too personally involved with her creation, Lord Peter, and there is little doubt of her disappointment at the critics' failure to accept the need to communicate more in a detective novel than a clever puzzle and its solution. In the twenty years between *Busman's honeymoon* and her death, no new Lord Peter novels were produced.

In the case of Agatha Christie, there has been no noticeable attempt to do other than tell a good story, to baffle her readers with ingenuity and sleight of hand. She has used every trick in the book, or so it always seems until her next novel appears! Possibly other writers have written more erudite detective stories, or have shown greater skill in characterisation. None, however, have sustained a comparably high standard of the conjuror's art throughout more than fifty years. Only Mrs Christie can make this claim. While we may long for the days of Roger Ackroyd, her stroke of genius published in 1926, she is even now capable of staggering her readers with a new twist.

Her first detective novel was

> CHRISTIE Agatha
> The mysterious affair at Styles. A detective story
> John Lane 1920

which, although not her most accomplished, is significant in that it introduced Hercule Poirot. The dapper Belgian with the tidy mind, who solves cases by exercising his 'little grey cells', is arguably the best known fictional sleuth since Sherlock Holmes. He makes his first appearance in an Essex village, where old Mrs Inglethorp dies from strychnine poisoning. In the tradition which Agatha Christie was to make her own, the field of suspects is restricted, but this does not diminish the degree of surprise when a particularly unpleasant murderer is finally unmasked.

Generally regarded as the author's *tour de force*,

CHRISTIE Agatha
The murder of Roger Ackroyd
Collins 1926

holds a unique position in the history of detective fiction. This is because of its highly original use of one particular technique, which transforms it from a run-of-the-mill whodunit to something special. The technique, although subsequently copied by many writers, has never again been so adroitly achieved. Agatha Christie was accused of 'cheating' by several critics, but others including Dorothy L Sayers came to her defence. Even at this stage it would be churlish to reveal who killed Roger Ackroyd, as the special satisfaction of reading this book has yet to be experienced by new generations of enthusiasts. But from the moment Hercule Poirot comes out of temporary retirement in the village of Kings Abbot to investigate this case of murder and blackmail, any reader who fails to question the meaning of everything Mrs Christie says will only have himself to blame.

Another highly ingenious plot from the pen of Agatha Christie,

CHRISTIE Agatha
Murder on the Orient Express
Collins 1934

was recently given a new lease of life by a highly successful film adaptation with an international cast. The famed Orient Express on this particular journey has a motley assortment of passengers, including Hercule Poirot and a child-murderer. The train comes to a halt, snowbound. The child-murderer is found dead in his berth, stabbed with most unusual ferocity. Which of the passengers could have been guilty of such a crime, Poirot asks, and could it be that they have something in common?

Mrs Ascher at Andover . . . Betty Barnard at Bexhill . . . Sir Carmichael Clarke at Churston . . . One by one

CHRISTIE Agatha
The ABC murders
Collins 1936

are committed and an 'ABC railway guide' is left by each victim – surely the work of a maniac? But the killer's first mistake is to challenge Hercule Poirot, whose ability as a detective is matched only by his supreme vanity. Accompanied by the rather silly Captain Hastings, as in most of his early cases, Poirot is in brilliant form in his pursuit of the ABC murderer. The solution is logical yet unexpected.

Not all of Agatha Christie's books feature Hercule Poirot. Her other principal detective, the elderly Miss Jane Marple, appears in many cases. On the whole, however, it is Poirot who has appeared in her most memorable novels. There have also been some in which no central detective character has appeared, perhaps the best known of these being

> CHRISTIE Agatha
> Ten little niggers
> Collins 1939

Subsequently adapted for stage and screen – although the book itself is even more accomplished – this story starts conventionally enough, with ten unconnected people being invited to an island by a host who apparently fails to materialise. But then they are murdered one by one, like the old nursery rhyme. It becomes clear that their mysterious host is in fact one of them, and furthermore they are cut off from the mainland.

In another novel without a series detective,

> CHRISTIE Agatha
> The pale horse
> Collins 1961

the question posed is whether it is possible for murder to be committed by remote control, not by any mechanical device but by something like telepathy. This is the implication of a list of apparently random names found on the body of a murdered priest – the common factor is that they all died extremely suddenly. The pace and excitement of this novel, combined with its sting in the tail, are sufficient to demonstrate that one does not need to go back to the twenties and thirties for examples of the Christie genius. This one is among her best.

And finally, for those readers who yearn for the early days of Hercule Poirot and his rather dull confidant Hastings, a recent collection of short stories

> CHRISTIE Agatha
> Poirot's early cases
> Collins 1974

contains eighteen excellent examples of the little Belgian at work. With one exception, *The Market Basing mystery*, none of the stories have appeared in book form in Britain previously. 'Pure chance,' begins the first story, 'led my friend Hercule Poirot . . . to be connected with the Styles case.' And so we have come full circle.

In Margery Allingham (1904–1966) there was something more akin to Sayers than to Christie. Her fame dates from the publication of

ALLINGHAM Margery
Death of a ghost
William Heinemann 1934

in which, unlike her earlier novels, the mystery puzzle is set against a background which is authentically conveyed and impressions of the social scene flow from the Allingham pen in a manner which was to make her mark. In contrast with Agatha Christie, the whodunit element is not necessarily always the most important aspect, although Miss Allingham was still a superbly competent practitioner. What she lacked in the Christie sleight of hand was more than rectified by her exquisite character drawing and her devastating thumbnail portraits.

In *Death of a ghost*, the unlikely murder scene is the fashionable annual exhibition of the work of John Sebastian Lafcadio R A, organised by his widow and art dealer Max Fustian. A distinguished gathering of art enthusiasts and poseurs, finely drawn by the penetrating Miss Allingham, are on the spot when Tommy Dacre is stabbed, but Inspector Stanislaus Oates does not find this particularly helpful. Luckily Mr Campion is on hand too. Albert Campion, 'a lank, pale-faced young man with sleek fair hair and horn-rimmed spectacles . . . well-bred and a trifle absent-minded', is the mainstay of Margery Allingham's detective novels. He bears certain resemblances to Lord Peter Wimsey and to Ngaio Marsh's Roderick Alleyn, at least in respect of his dilettantism and aristocratic connections.

Another of Albert Campion's well known cases,

ALLINGHAM Margery
Dancers in mourning
William Heinemann 1937

finds him investigating a series of vicious practical jokes which have been plaguing dancer Jimmy Sutane. At Sutane's country house it is clear that murderous intent lurks beneath the facade of theatrical matyness which his guests display, and death occurs in an atmosphere of tension which Miss Allingham conveys faultlessly.

Miss Allingham's perception and insight, particularly in matters psychological, are much in evidence in a collection of short stories entitled

ALLINGHAM Margery
Mr Campion and others
William Heinemann 1939

Bespectacled Mr Campion has a large circle of acquaintances, many of whom seem only too eager to involve him in their problems. Be they questions of blackmail, robbery or worse, the combination of Campion and Stanislaus Oates of Scotland Yard is one which meets with considerable success. The stories are clever, eminently readable, and with that touch of social satire which gives them spice.

Probably the most unusual Allingham novel, and arguably her best in some respects, is

ALLINGHAM Margery
The tiger in the smoke
Chatto & Windus 1952

A truly outstanding work, and somewhat outside her style of earlier years, this shows Margery Allingham's almost uncanny ability to create atmosphere. Here it is the atmosphere of London, the smoke of the title. Whether the characters are sinister or salt-of-the-earth, from a group of buskers to a canon, the author's artistry in characterisation is yet again demonstrated. Basically it is a novel of suspense rather than a detective story, a fast moving journey as we pursue the trail of Jack Havoc – the tiger – following his escape from prison. Many of the regular Allingham characters are involved, including Albert Campion, his man Lugg, and Stanislaus Oates, the latter incidentally having progressed from Inspector to Assistant Commissioner since *Death of a ghost*. It may be felt that Albert Campion is superfluous on this occasion, that this particular novel can stand on its own, and indeed the film adaptation of *The tiger in the smoke* omitted him.

The last in this quartet of Queens of Crime, Ngaio Marsh, has a long list of books to her credit. Like Miss Allingham she displays far more than the ability to devise a clever puzzle. Her detective, now Superintendent Alleyn, is one of the acknowledged greats of crime fiction. One of the classics of the genre is

MARSH Ngaio
Artists in crime
Geoffrey Bles 1938

in which Alleyn investigates the murder of a model at the home of

54

Agatha Troy R A. Miss Troy's art students are a motley gathering, and somewhere among their interpersonal relationships lies the motive for murder. This competent novel, with the artistic background well portrayed, also introduces Alleyn to his future wife. The romance and marriage of Alleyn and Agatha Troy span Ngaio Marsh's novels, just as Dorothy L Sayers combined crime with the romantic affairs of Lord Peter and Harriet Vane.

There is no disagreement among the critics concerning the excellence of

MARSH Ngaio
Overture to death
Collins 1939

It is Saturday night in the parish hall at Winton St Giles, and the audience is about to enjoy a play. Miss Idris Campanula takes her seat at the piano to perform the overture – Rachmaninoff's Prelude in C sharp minor. It begins with the familiar Pom Pom POM. Then Miss Campanula's foot comes down on the soft pedal. At this point there is a report from the revolver which someone has carefully arranged in the piano, and Miss Campanula has a bullet hole in her head. Such an ingenious way to commit a murder calls for the intellectual capabilities of Chief Detective-Inspector Roderick Alleyn.

In the case of

MARSH Ngaio
Surfeit of Lampreys
Collins 1941

the principal claim to fame lies in its impeccable, credible and finely etched characters. This is a good example of a detective novel which is also a creditable piece of literature. The members of the Lamprey family will be remembered by many readers, long after they have forgotten the details of the crime itself – the particularly nasty stabbing of the Marquis of Wutherwood and Rune in a lift. Fortunately Roderick Alleyn is at hand, accompanied by his usual retinue from Scotland Yard. But it must be repeated that it is the brilliant portrayal of the Lampreys, rather than the plot, which makes this one of the best detective novels ever.

Another of Miss Marsh's notable features is her ability to make the setting complementary to the plot, and several of her novels demonstrate to perfection how settings can be far more than just a backcloth against which a murder mystery is enacted. The world of the theatre, amateur and professional, she has used on several occasions. One of her most original, however, is

MARSH Ngaio
Died in the wool
Collins 1945

which uses a sheep station in her native New Zealand as an unusual locale for one of Alleyn's most interesting cases. The corpse of Florence Rubrick, a Member of Parliament who has been missing for some weeks, is found in a bale of wool at a textile manufactory. Alleyn, not accompanied this time by his assistants from the Yard, confines the mystery to Mount Moon sheep station and to Mrs Rubrick's circle of family and friends. The problem is aggravated by the fact that the murder is already more than one year old before Alleyn comes on the scene.

This look at the four Queens of Crime can only end with an unanswered question. Will any of the women detective novelists of today ever aspire to such a title? Only time will tell. One certainty, however, is that the collected works of Sayers, Christie, Allingham and Marsh would constitute, if gathered together, all that is best in detective fiction from the twenties to the present day. They provide a fitting example for the future.

6 Detection in the thirties, forties and fifties

Although in the nineteen thirties various attempts were made to break away from the traditional detective story, there were still considerable numbers being produced. Indeed the same still applies today. There has always been ample scope for innovations, and neither the psychological crime novel nor the hardboiled and laconic private eye story have put the cosy puzzle out of business.

Two of the breakaway trends will be covered in sections 7 and 8. In this section we shall remain with the pure detective story, and pinpoint some of the writers who produced excellent material in the thirties, forties and fifties.

This period, still a Golden Age by any standards, saw a wide range of highly ingenious detective fiction on both sides of the Atlantic. There was a fascinating mixture of different approaches, including locked room mysteries, the donnish school, and more exponents of the much-maligned 'Had I But Known' technique.

During the 1920s, Ronald A Knox formulated rules governing the art of the detective story, on the grounds that there must be a fair game played between the author and the reader. These rules appeared in a Preface to *Best detective stories* (Faber 1929) edited by Knox and H Harrington. They were later reproduced, with a commentary, in the essay entitled 'Detective Stories' in his *Literary distractions* (Sheed & Ward 1958).

Many writers of the thirties, forties and fifties adhered to the Knox rules, but even those who bent them a little were creating work with its own peculiar fascination.

Philip MacDonald, for example, could at times demonstrate the features of classic detective fiction, then sometimes cross into the field of the macabre, and on other occasions he produced plots little short of farce. Although born in London and writing with an English flavour, he went comparatively early in his career to the USA and has been responsible for many Hollywood scripts. His first novel featuring Anthony Gethryn was published as early as 1924, but

MACDONALD Philip

The rasp. A detective story
Collins 1924

is still regarded as a classic of the genre, although present day critics
might be so impressed by the ingenuity of some of MacDonald's successors that they now underrate his abilities. Firstly, MacDonald
could write well, as befits a member of a literary family; his father was
novelist and playwright Ronald MacDonald, and his grandfather was
the Scottish poet and novelist George MacDonald. Secondly, his
superb variations on certain techniques of detective fiction placed him
high on the list of greats, particularly during the twenties and thirties,
and although not primarily an innovator he devised improvements
and added new twists which stamped almost every MacDonald novel
as very much his own.

In *The rasp* we see that basically it uses the well worn theme of 'body
in the study at his country residence'. But this is only the beginning,
and MacDonald adds his own special dashes of humour, touches of
the macabre, and Gethryn working inexorably to a surprise climax in
true Golden Age tradition.

Following the publication of *The rasp* MacDonald went from
strength to strength. He specialised in snappy titles. One of them,

MACDONALD Philip
The noose
Collins 1930

was the first Crime Club selection and highly praised by Arnold Bennett. Under the pseudonym 'Martin Porlock' he produced

PORLOCK Martin
X v Rex
Collins 1933

which appeared in later editions under his own name. It begins when
an unknown murderer kills a police sergeant at his station desk. This
is quickly followed by the strangling of a constable and the stabbing of
another. It soon becomes apparent that the mysterious X is a maniac
whose series of crimes is likely to extend indefinitely, and the case creates a national problem of cabinet proportions. Novels containing a
considerable number of murders run the risk of becoming mono-
tonous and losing the reader's interest because of obvious artificiality.
This is one of the few examples where this sacrifice is not made, which
marks it as a *tour de force*.

The talents of MacDonald are to be seen in many short stories in
addition to his excellent novels. The collection entitled

MACDONALD Philip
The man out of the rain, and other stories
Herbert Jenkins 1957
reveals his many facets – his mastery of suspense, the knockout
climax, the combination of humour and horror, and in general his
technique as a superior craftsman in the art of storytelling. There are
six stories here, and we are reminded more than ever of the author's
association in Hollywood with such giants of the film industry as
Alfred Hitchcock.

MacDonald's output thinned during the forties and fifties, presumably as his film work increased, but as recently as 1960 he produced
what must rank as one of his most interesting books,
MACDONALD Philip
The list of Adrian Messenger
Herbert Jenkins 1960
a strange novel the details of which it would be unfair to reveal here.
Let it merely be said that Major Messenger writes the names of ten
men on a slip of paper and gives it to a friend at Scotland Yard; that a
ruthless killer is the common factor between the names; and that
Anthony Gethryn finds this one of his most complex cases. Incidentally Gethryn was detecting throughout some thirty five years – and
he, like his creator, has been somewhat underrated. It would be a pity
if MacDonald's ingenuity and sense of fun were allowed to fall into
obscurity.

MacDonald's novels spanned a long period. Another of whom this
can be said, but whose best work appeared in the thirties, was Sir
Henry Aubrey-Fletcher (1887–1969). A soldier and civic dignitary,
Sir Henry wrote
WADE Henry
Policeman's lot: Stories of detection
Constable 1933
under the pseudonym which was to become well known. His work
had a quality shared by few, namely that he could write puzzle stories
which also depicted the life and work of police officers with a realism
for which he was noted. His policemen were hardly superhuman, and
indeed were often of comparatively lowly rank. One of his regular
characters, Detective Inspector Poole of Scotland Yard, appeared in
various novels but in *Policeman's lot* he is seen in top form as he persist-
ently unearths the facts and invariably alights upon those minute
matters of detail which murderers overlook. For good measure the

volume also contains six brilliant stories of the inverted variety, using techniques which were later to be effectively deployed in the works of such masters as Roy Vickers and Cyril Hare.

In a further collection of short stories,

WADE Henry
Here comes the copper
Constable 1938

we follow the career of a policeman called John Bragg. From the beat in Chelsea, where we see him in the first story, he proceeds to 'Downshire' and then returns to London as a detective constable in the CID. Each story bears Wade's authentic stamp, showing us the rough and the smooth of a copper's life. They are also excellent examples of the detective short story, well plotted, and in some cases relying upon small points of an ingenious nature which serve to trap villains.

If Henry Wade is no longer a household name, that surely can not be said of John Dickson Carr. It is virtually impossible to select the 'best' novel from his considerable output, written under his own name and as 'Carter Dickson'. His list of locked room mysteries was phenomenal and no other writer has devised more variations on this particular theme. Most of them have a horrific or quasi-supernatural atmosphere which generally turns out to have been deliberately manufactured by the murderer.

CARR John Dickson
The hollow man
Hamish Hamilton 1935

is a good example of this, presenting several 'impossible' crimes which only the true connoisseur will come within a mile of unravelling. Another nice touch is that one chapter provides the Chestertonian Dr Gideon Fell with an opportunity to discourse upon the various methods by which locked room murders may be committed. Mr Carr seems not to have minded revealing these secrets – his subsequent career was to show that he had dozens of alternative solutions in mind.

Another typical example of his work is

DICKSON Carter
The Plague Court murders
William Heinemann 1935

which presents a combination of the supernatural and the seemingly impossible murder. In a room which apparently no living creature can have entered, a fake spiritualist is brutally murdered. As with all locked room mysteries, the identity of the killer is only part of the puzzle and the deductive skill of the reader is taxed even more by the question of how it was done. The massive and eccentric detective Sir Henry Merrivale solves it, and the author plays scrupulously fair.

The detective novels of Georgette Heyer (1902–1974) have been somewhat obscured by the popularity of her numerous historical romances, and her name is scarcely ever mentioned as one of the more competent crime writers. This is a pity, for she produced many neat puzzles in the classic form, mostly during the thirties. One of the best,

HEYER Georgette
Death in the stocks
Longmans 1935

was published in the USA under the title *Merely murder*. The village stocks at Ashleigh Green are a well known feature, but Constable Dickenson sees them in use for the first time when he discovers the body of Arnold Vereker. Mr Vereker, a weekend visitor to a local cottage, is not short of people who stand to profit by his death. There are many possible motives, which it is the lot of Superintendent Hannasyde to unravel. Considering her plotting ability, her nice touches of comedy, and better than average characterisation, Georgette Heyer has been sadly neglected as a crime writer.

Not all classics of the thirties were of the intellectual variety. The novels of Ethel Lina White were cast somewhat in the mould of Mary Roberts Rinehart, in view of the fact that the reader is often invited to associate with a helpless woman in danger. The one title which succeeds admirably in this intention is

WHITE Ethel Lina
The wheel spins
Collins 1936

Its effectiveness and its memorability stem from the fact that anyone – especially the reader – might easily have the same experience on a train as heroine Iris Carr. This very ordinariness of the situation, with small everyday items gradually beginning to assume sinister significance, is the very stuff of which Hitchcock films are made – indeed this novel was successfully adapted for the screen as *The lady vanishes*, and the current edition by Hamish Hamilton bears this title. The story of how Iris Carr met the chatty governess Miss Froy on a train is brimfull of menace. Miss Froy disappears, and her fellow travellers all deny that she ever existed. Poor tortured Iris begins to feel that she must have imagined her conversation with the harmless little lady, but various small pieces of evidence indicate otherwise.

There can be no greater difference in style and content than that between the works of Ethel Lina White and two other crime writers whose careers began simultaneously with the publication of *The wheel spins*. The early contributions of 'Michael Innes' and 'Nicholas Blake' will be considered next.

J I M Stewart, academic and novelist, has produced a considerable number of detective novels and thrillers since the thirties under the pseudonym 'Michael Innes'. It is on his first few titles that his reputation is securely based. Together with 'Nicholas Blake' and 'Edmund Crispin', he brought a new literacy and intellectualism to a field which had become increasingly humdrum. Too many writers were relying upon the dull formula whereby the detective systematically interviews all the suspects, and then minutely sifts all the points of the various alibis; other writers were setting out deliberately to produce lighthearted works of the 'what fun, here's a body' variety. Innes played a large part in pulling detective fiction out of the rut, but it must not be assumed that his work was in any way pretentious. He intended to write *detective* novels, not novels 'with detective interruptions' like Dorothy L Sayers.

Let anyone who feels that the employment of good English is wasted in the field of crime fiction pay careful attention to Mr Innes' early works, where literary craftsmanship and the ability to devise ingenious plots are equally apparent. His first was

INNES Michael
Death at the president's lodging
Victor Gollancz 1936

which was described in *The times literary supplement* as 'the most important contribution to detective literature that has appeared for some time'. This debut by Inspector John Appleby, who many novels later became Sir John, concerns the murder of the president of St Anthony's College. Only the fellows had keys to his lodging, and so Appleby appears to have a neat and confined group of suspects. Moreover the detective is not by any means faced with a wall of silence, as scandals and passions incline the fellows toward self protection and to produce evidence against their colleagues. The acclaim given to this first book was exceeded on the publication of his second, intriguingly entitled

INNES Michael
Hamlet, revenge! A story in four parts

Victor Gollancz 1937

in which Appleby investigates the murder of the Lord Chancellor at the Duke of Horton's country seat, Scamnum Court. A private pro duction of *Hamlet* sets the scene, and it is during the performance that the murder is committed. Appleby is, as usual, urbane and brimfull of literary allusions – his penchant for swapping quotations with the best of them has followed him throughout his career, giving him an erudition which few readers should find as irritating as, say, the pseudo chitchat of Philo Vance or Lord Peter Wimsey. Possibly it is because Appleby is unobtrusive, so unaggressively normal, that he has survived the passage of time.

Michael Innes, significantly with only two books published, was received by *The times literary supplement* as 'in a class by himself among writers of detective fiction', but any bibliography of the best in the field must include all of his first three, and the third,

INNES Michael
Lament for a maker
Victor Gollancz 1938

is generally recognised as his supreme achievement. Scotland is the setting, and Appleby is again investigating a murder, although he does not make his appearance until some considerable way through the book. The unusual feature is that each part is narrated by one of the principal characters, and the style varies from one to another. Innes succeeds beautifully in conveying the feel of Scotland through his characters. In particular the prose of Ewan Bell, shoemaker of Kinkeig and elder of the Kirk, has a richness very few contemporary writers can convey. This must surely rank as one of the most beautifully written detective novels of all time.

'Nicholas Blake' was another who brought a new literacy and a donnish flavour to the detective novel. He was, as is generally known, the late Poet Laureate C Day Lewis (1904–1972). The quality of his books, maintained over many years, was further evidence of the fact that literary credentials of the highest standing were not wasted in the fields of straight detection, the thriller and the spy story, for he produced excellent examples of these forms. It was the classic whodunit, however, to which he paid most attention. His first was

BLAKE Nicholas
A question of proof
Collins 1935

and it received considerable critical acclaim, among the enthusiasts being Dorothy L Sayers and Sir Hugh Walpole. Of the multitude of murder mysteries which have been set in boys' schools, it is likely that top honours should go to this debut by Nicholas Blake. An unpopular boy named Wemyss is found strangled at Sudeley Hall preparatory school, and it is likely that one of the staff is the murderer. Unlike Michael Innes, Blake leaves his cases in the hands of an amateur detective, and the appearance of Nigel Strangeways at Sudeley Hall was a turning point in crime fiction, introducing a character who was to hold a significant position on the roll of honour. From the outset he is portrayed as something of a rebel, having left university after answering his mods papers in limericks, because 'the spectacle of so many quite decent youths being got at and ruined for life was too much for him'. Physically he is described as 'like one of the less successful busts of T E Lawrence', and he is a man of many fads.

His problems at Sudeley Hall are considerable, and culminate in a second murder, but the main difficulty is proving the identity of the murderer even when he is sure of it. Although *A question of proof* is not Blake's outstanding achievement, it heralded a career of major proportions. Another of his earliest novels,

BLAKE Nicholas
The beast must die
Collins 1938

is generally regarded as his most accomplished book. A mixture of detection and psychological suspense, it may be compared with the work of Francis Iles and yet still ranks as an exercise in deduction. 'I am going to kill a man. I don't know his name, I don't know where he lives, I have no idea what he looks like.' These are the opening words of a book which should be required reading for every enthusiast.

Devotees of detective fiction will have their own particular favourites among the novels featuring Nigel Strangeways.

BLAKE Nicholas
Minute for murder
Collins 1947

is one of special ingenuity, set in the 'Ministry of Morale' during wartime. A cyanide capsule, taken from a captured Nazi chief, disappears but is soon put to use. An attractive secretary is poisoned in front of seven witnesses, and fortunately Nigel Strangeways is one of them. The difficulty of establishing a motive, and the unearthing of office and extramural relationships, are problems which Strangeways has to take in his stride in this highly competent piece of classic detective fiction.

Slightly later on the scene, but very much associated with the breakthrough started by Innes and Blake, was 'Edmund Crispin'. Under his own name, Bruce Montgomery, he is a successful composer particularly known for his film music. The Crispin pseudonym was employed for eight fine detective novels, followed in 1953 by a volume of short stories, *Beware of the trains* (Victor Gollancz). Since then the Crispin name has occurred regularly as one of the foremost reviewers of detective fiction and as a crime and science fiction anthologist. In his first novel

CRISPIN Edmund
The case of the gilded fly
Victor Gollancz 1944

we are introduced to Gervase Fen, Professor of English Language and Literature in the University of Oxford. Fen is a character who tends always to be around when murder is committed, and on this occasion the obnoxious Yseut Haskell is done to death on Fen's home patch, in one of the colleges no less. The action alternates between the university and the Oxford Repertory Theatre, as befits the Crispin forte of the academic and the literary. Ever a curious one, and interspersing the action with his own brand of pungent comment, Fen concludes a highly entertaining novel with a theatrical exposure of the murderer. One of Crispin's strong points is his ability to bring wit, satire even, to the detective novel. He displays a sense of fun which might occasionally be facetious, and he reminds us that it is all a story and should not be confused with real life – but he never descends to low farce. A special example of his comic approach is

CRISPIN Edmund
The moving toyshop. A detective story
Victor Gollancz 1946

which is his most highly regarded book, although all his novels are well worth reading. Again set in Oxford, it provides poet Richard Cadogan with an unlikely problem. Cadogan discovers a strangled corpse in a toyshop at midnight, but when he returns with the police the shop has disappeared. Although this immediately types him as a madman, Cadogan is fortunately acquainted with Gervase Fen, and together they set out in hilarious pursuit. Perhaps on reflection this *is* farce, but intelligent farce for all that.

Another writer of distinction was Gordon Clark (1900–1958), who combined a career as a detective novelist with a busy legal practice which culminated in his appointment as a county court judge. Using the pseudonym 'Cyril Hare' he wrote a handful of excellent detective novels and some superlative short stories, his best known book being

HARE Cyril
Tragedy at law
Faber & Faber 1942

This stands out as much for the realistic portrayal of a judge on circuit as for its puzzle plot, and is indeed accepted as the classic among detective novels with a legal setting. It may be compared with some of the best work of Dorothy L Sayers for its combination of detection, manners, and authentic background – except that here we have barrister Francis Pettigrew investigating, instead of the often irritating Lord Peter Wimsey. It would be churlish to reveal details of the plot, as even the identity of the murder victim is not easily foreseeable. Suffice it to say that it is a satisfying novel which will remain a detective fiction cornerstone.

Cyril Hare also wrote a considerable number of short stories, and

Best detective stories of Cyril Hare. Chosen with an introduction by Michael Gilbert
Faber & Faber 1959

is an excellent collection containing first class examples of the art. Many of them are extremely short – four pages or so – and revolve around the one small point which gives a murderer away. In this respect some of them have a likeness to the rather longer stories of Roy Vickers. There are comparatively few masters of the crime short story; it is an unusually difficult form avoided by many writers in spite of the fact that, if we remember Poe, it was the original form of the genre. Cyril Hare's are among the shortest and the best.

Although policemen figured largely in detective novels from their outset, the police novel as such was virtually unknown until Maurice Procter entered the field. More recently there have been examples such as J J Marric and John Wainwright. The method which Procter followed, and probably initiated, was that the mainspring of the book was not a crime, but the documentary treatment of police work. We see in Procter's work the relationships within the force, the conflicts between policemen as individuals and their duties to the community. Having pursued a long career as a policeman himself, he knows all the facts and we see a policeman's life down to the last detail. In his best known book,

PROCTER Maurice

No proud chivalry

Longmans, Green 1946 (Now Chivers – New Portway Reprints)

he follows the progress of one Pierce Rogan from the day he joins the Otherburn Borough Police as a constable. One can almost smell the boot leather.

Four exceptional writers were mentioned in the separate section on Queens of Crime, but there have of course been many other women who have contributed substantially to the development of crime fiction. Some, although they did not have the impact of the four mentioned earlier, have nonetheless produced competent work which has enjoyed some popularity and kept up a good standard of craftsmanship. Georgette Heyer has already been mentioned, and two other writers worthy of note are Gladys Mitchell and Josephine Tey.

Gladys Mitchell has produced a large number of detective novels since the 1920s featuring the eccentric figure of Mrs Beatrice Lestrange Bradley. She has a nose for a mystery and a screech like a parrot. Most of the Mrs Bradley novels are whodunits of a high standard, and a representative title of more than average readability is

MITCHELL Gladys

Tom Brown's body

Michael Joseph 1949

Set in a boys' public school, as so many good detective stories seem to be, it concerns the murder of an unpopular junior master. It is clear that boys and masters know considerably more than they are prepared to admit, and it is fortunate indeed that Mrs Bradley is staying at that time in the village. From researching into witchcraft, as is her wont, she takes time off to investigate.

The comparatively small output of Elizabeth Mackintosh (1897–1952) as 'Josephine Tey' ranged from classic detection to the modern reconstruction of historical *causes célèbres*. It is extremely difficult to choose one of her works to describe as her major achievement, but most authorities would cite

TEY Josephine

The daughter of time

Peter Davies 1951

as outstanding for its novelty. Inspector Alan Grant is forced into the role of armchair detective in a literal sense when he is hospitalised after a fall. The case he chooses to occupy his mind is one which has intrigued many others before him. He reaches a solution

– not necessarily a very original one – but only after following up some fruitful lines of research. The case is one of the longest standing unsolved murders, that of the princes in the Tower.

Michael Gilbert, who edited the volume of Cyril Hare stories quoted earlier, is no mean exponent of detective stories himself. His work is typified by good writing, a neat eye for characterisation, and liberal dashes of humour which should suit those who like their detective novels on the lighter side. He has in fact covered a wide range from the classical detective form to the novel of action. His settings too have varied widely, and have in all cases been realistically conveyed. In

GILBERT Michael
Smallbone deceased
Hodder & Stoughton 1950

the corpse is found in a solicitor's office of authentic impeccability, no doubt attributable to the author's own legal background. It is found, moreover, in a hermetically sealed deedbox, and to find the murderer among the mixed bag of somewhat eccentric people connected with the firm presents a daunting prospect for Inspector Hazlerigg and Henry Bohun.

GILBERT Michael
Death in captivity
Hodder & Stoughton 1952

is another of Gilbert's novels which has carved a special niche for itself. A combination of murder mystery and prisoner-of-war escape story, it is a skilful portrayal of men within a tense environment. The atmosphere of an Italian POW camp is well conveyed.

It is known that the field of detective fiction is rich in curiosities. Most of them, though interesting, do not warrant inclusion in a list of 'the best'. In view of the popularity of Sherlock Holmes, however, and his influence upon the development of the genre, special notice must be given to

DOYLE Adrian Conan and CARR John Dickson
The exploits of Sherlock Holmes
John Murray 1954

This combination of the inside knowledge of Sir Arthur's son and the skill of a top storyteller with an uncanny knack of conveying the Victorian atmosphere, results in just the sort of tales one would expect. They are of a good standard, and written in simulation of the original style. The plots are new, and each is based upon cases to which Dr Watson makes passing reference in the original stories. Although the complete Holmes fanatic might disagree, the task is pulled off rather well.

Turning to the thirties in the USA, the first really major name which occurs is that of 'Ellery Queen'. If one were to list the top four or so 'all time greats' of American mystery fiction, it must inevitably include this name. Two cousins, Frederic Dannay and Manfred B Lee, collaborated under this pseudonym when in 1929 they produced

QUEEN Ellery
The Roman hat mystery
New York Stokes 1929; Victor Gollancz 1929

Their first half dozen novels were written very much to a series format. The titles are on series lines, and a 'Challenge to the reader' appears at the end of each book at the point at which all the clues are in the reader's possession. The detection is of the classic English variety, although this is not to detract from the superb plotting skill and a crafty inventiveness that few writers have equalled.

Ellery Queen is in fact the amateur detective hero of the series, aiding and abetting (and putting to shame) his father, Inspector Richard Queen. The books are populated by patently wooden characters; as with many classic detective novels, the early output of Ellery Queen puts puzzle before character analysis, and indeed Ellery himself can only be described as a figure of somewhat irritating mannerisms. As Dannay and Lee progressed, however, their work was gradually transformed from the pure detective novel to something approaching the crime novel as we know it today. Possibly they were influenced by developments in the field generally. Their best known works are nevertheless their earliest cases featuring Ellery and his 'famous analytico-deductive method', and highly recommended is

QUEEN Ellery
The Greek coffin mystery
New York Stokes 1932; Victor Gollancz 1932

The activities of Ellery Queen were as celebrated in the short form as in the full length novel.

QUEEN Ellery
The adventures of Ellery Queen. Problems in deduction
New York Stokes 1934; Victor Gollancz 1935

is a noteworthy collection consisting of eleven investigations which display the perfect blend of puzzle and pace, with just a dash of horror. Detective short stories by Queen, according to John Dickson Carr, are 'in a class by themselves'.

The thirties also saw the emergence of another great 'character' detective, Mr Moto. John P Marquand (1893–1960) introduced him in a series of novels which can be categorised as secret service tales rather than pure detection, but there are more than a few detective elements included and Mr Moto himself is somewhat akin to his Chinese counterpart Charlie Chan. Earl Derr Biggers was writing some ten years earlier, but the appearance of the Japanese Mr Moto must for many readers have seemed a welcome reincarnation of one of their favourite fictional detectives. Moto is, of course, inscrutable and razor witted. The novels, set in the mystic Far East, are liberally larded with political intrigue and murder. And Mr Moto, small and chunky, murmurs 'so sorry' and other stock phrases while completely pulling the wool over the villains' eyes.

John P Marquand, acclaimed for his straight novels, originally wrote the Moto stories for *The saturday evening post* after spending some time in the orient. The omnibus volume

MARQUAND John P
Mr Moto's three aces
Boston Little, Brown 1956

contains *Thank you, Mr Moto* (Boston Little, Brown 1936; Herbert Jenkins 1937), *Think fast, Mr Moto* (Boston Little, Brown 1937; Robert Hale 1938) and *Mr Moto is so sorry* (Boston Little, Brown 1938; Robert Hale 1939).

One of the most difficult techniques is that of combining detection with farce. Few writers have succeeded in this, but a notable exception was Phoebe Atwood Taylor. Her novel

TAYLOR Phoebe Atwood
The Cape Cod mystery
Indianapolis Bobbs-Merrill 1931

with homespun detective Asey Mayo, was particularly praised in its time. Her best series, however, was written under the pseudonym 'Alice Tilton'. They feature a most original detective, Leonidas Witherall. He is a gently unassuming academic who also happens to bear a striking physical resemblance to Shakespeare. In the first, bearing the unlikely title

TILTON Alice
Beginning with a bash
Collins 1937

the musty calm of Peters' second-hand bookstore is shattered when

Professor North is killed by a blow to the skull. Luckily 'Bill Shakespeare' is on hand, and he pursues a characteristically mirthful course to the solution. Although an apparent contradiction, the Witherall stories are a very 'English' brand of detection by an American writer.

The early novels of Mignon G Eberhart were examples of the 'Had I But Known' school founded by Mary Roberts Rinehart, although she later developed into the field of the psychological suspense novel. Hospital and nursing home settings were her particular forte. In spite of her association with the Rinehart school, Mrs Eberhart produced some excellent novels blending detection with a touch of terror. One of her most popular and memorable characters is Susan Dare, who appears in

EBERHART Mignon G
The cases of Susan Dare
New York Doubleday, Doran 1934; John Lane 1935

Susan is a typical young heroine, charming and somewhat emotional, and displaying understandable horror at being caught up in situations involving murder in menacing locations. She is a writer of mystery stories who, together with gallant young reporter Jim Byrne, has a knack of getting involved in murder at the drop of a hat. The six stories in this collection contain some nice ingenious touches, and are a pleasant mixture of whodunit and hair raiser.

A character who was to become something of an institution also made his debut in the thirties. Perry Mason proved to be one of the most popular characters in detective fiction, and his popularity was enhanced by the long running television series. Erle Stanley Gardner (1889–1970) produced the books very much to a pattern, and with surprising rapidity – the first three were published in the USA in 1933. The plots were entertaining, the characters cardboard, and in short they were nothing more than a good, enjoyable read. Erle Stanley Gardner's legal experience, and his work for the pulp magazines, meant that he had vast experience behind him when he launched this series of courtroom dramas. In each of them, lawyer Mason uses all his wily skills and just-legal chicanery, invariably pulling off the acquittal of his client and the exposure of the murderer in the final pages.

GARDNER Erle Stanley
The case of the sulky girl
New York Morrow 1933; Harrap 1934

is a very early example, concerning a beautiful girl who is worried about her father's will. When the trustee has his head beaten in, her problems are only just beginning.

From the characters of Erle Stanley Gardner, who are little more than ciphers, it is a far cry to the work of Rex Stout and his larger-than-life creation Nero Wolfe. Gourmet, beer drinker and orchid fancier, the massive Wolfe made his first appearance in

STOUT Rex
Fer-de-lance
New York Farrar & Rinehart 1934; Cassell 1935

and forty years later is still on the crime fiction scene. An armchair detective in the literal sense, Wolfe moves as rarely as possible from his study out of deference to both his immense weight and his superior intellect. Naturally he interviews suspects and searches for clues, but he does this through his young legman Archie Goodwin, who incidentally is one of the most active and catalytic 'Watsons' in the history of crime fiction. A considerable number of Nero Wolfe novels have appeared, but apart from being the first *Fer-de-lance* is also a nearly perfect example of detection at its purest, as Wolfe exercises his ego and his infallibility upon the case of Professor Barstow, who drops dead while playing golf.

There is humour in the Nero Wolfe stories, but they are not generally regarded as comic detective novels. The latter are difficult to produce, but Elliot Paul (1891–1958) was highly successful with the satirical bordering on the zany stories featuring Homer Evans. Homer is a tall, broad shouldered playboy with a seemingly inexhaustible range of talents. In his first case,

PAUL Elliot
The mysterious Mickey Finn, or Murder at the Café du Dôme.
An international mystery
New York Modern Age Books 1939; Penguin 1953

he is in search of a disappearing millionaire in a romp in the Parisian artists' quarter. The author's introduction sets the tone, in which he apologises for the absence of corpses in the first few pages, but warns that 'the casualties are going to be fairly heavy before we get through'.

Not just lighthearted but downright crazy, the work of Elliot Paul is in a class of its own. Perhaps on reconsideration one should also admit to that class Georgina Ann Randolph, who used the pseudonym 'Craig Rice'. Another exponent of the zany school of detection, she wrote novels featuring street photographers cum detectives Bingo and Handsome which are prime examples of knockabout comedy murder.

72

But it is
>RICE Craig
>Trial by fury
>New York Simon & Schuster 1941; Hammond, Hammond
>1950

on which her excellent reputation is founded. Jackson County, with its first murders for thirty two years, is a small community setting with some well drawn characters. Jake and Helene Justus, together with lawyer J J Malone, dig beneath the surface respectability in their search for the killer. Toughness and humour combined, without the forced wackyness of her later novels, place this in the forefront of Craig Rice's work.

No consideration of American detective fiction would be complete without Hugh C Wheeler and Richard W Webb, who collaborated under the pseudonyms Patrick Quentin, Q Patrick and Jonathan Stagge. Under the Quentin banner they wrote
>QUENTIN Patrick
>The man with two wives
>New York Simon & Schuster 1955; Victor Gollancz 1955

which is a strangely satisfying mixture of whodunit and psychological thriller. It deals with a dramatic situation in such a way that it comes over as perfectly credible. Bill Harding meets his ex-wife Angelica again, and finds she has become emotionally involved with a nasty piece of work called Jaimie Lumb. While Harding's second wife is out of town, Angelica visits him in the small hours – at the precise time, it seems, that Jaimie is being murdered. Can Harding give her an alibi, and risk his second marriage? To make matters worse, his rich father in law wants him to provide an alibi for someone else. And that is only the beginning of Harding's troubles. The whole complex story is narrated by the unfortunate Harding, totally innocent himself and yet caught like a fly in a web, and we follow his tortured thought processes. It is a *tour de force* with a surprise ending for good measure.

Having listed some works from Britain and the USA, there remains the question of European writers. Strange to tell, considering that Gaboriau was one of the people who started it all, continental detective novels have been few and far between. In the thirties to fifties there was really only one major French novelist translated into English in the field under discussion, Georges Simenon. He ranks, however, as world class.

Simenon's novels rival those of Edgar Wallace in sheer quantity, and a large proportion of them feature the solid, pipe smoking Inspector Maigret. In conception the early stories were influenced by the *romans policiers* of Emile Gaboriau, and the painstaking thoroughness of the early Maigret cases owed something also to Freeman Wills Crofts. But as his career developed Simenon displayed very much a style of his own. For one thing they are normally novelette length, with little time wasted on elaborate descriptive passages. Where such passages occur, they do not come over as part of the author's standard stock in trade. Rather are they impressions, atmospheres even, as sensed by Maigret himself. And they are the more realistic for this – if Paris has a distinctive smell, only Maigret communicates it to us.

Again, unlike many detectives, Maigret is no superman. He has a capacity for pity in no small degree. His methods are sometimes plodding, his humour is often cynical, and his success is frequently achieved by the possession of an innate sense of evil. He knows the frailties of human nature, and the criminal's compulsive desire to unburden his soul means that Maigret need only bide his time. We see him therefore as a patient man. So much so that two Maigret books with the same translated title appeared, and we are here concerned with

> SIMENON Georges
> The patience of Maigret. Translated . . . by Geoffrey Sainsbury
> G Routledge 1939

rather than the 1966 book of the same title. The former contains, as with many of the early books, two novelettes in one volume. These two, *A battle of nerves* and *A face for a clue* together present a perfect introduction to the early Maigret, with a flavour which perhaps the later stories did not quite achieve.

7   The hard boiled school

Rebellion against the quiet gentility of the classic detective story took various forms, one of which resulted in a whole new movement sometimes known as the hard boiled school.

It was an American movement, and its characters were tough, laconic, and infinitely more world-weary than the usual run of fictional detectives. They used guns and physical force more than intellectual reasoning, but this is not to say that the novels consisted purely of action packed incident. The best of them dig into the various forms of corruption in both high and low places, and secure our interest and sympathy by demonstrating that a situation is rarely all black or all white. This is normally seen through the eyes of a hard detective who, although capable of fighting fire with fire, is often also something of the philosopher.

The trends of detective fiction in the twenties and thirties were soundly rejected. The tendency to over elaborate was resisted, and the hard boiled school made little or no use of footnotes, diagrams, lists of characters, challenges to the reader, and the varied impedimenta of the English school. The crossword puzzle brigade, with their strict rules of the game, bore no relation to this gritty school which emerged in the USA from the early thirties.

'When in doubt, bring a man through the door with a gun!' was allegedly Raymond Chandler's answer to plotting difficulties. To this may be attributed the pace of Chandler's novels, and those of his fellow writers, but there is much more than this in the best of the hard boiled school. The work of Hammett, Chandler and others frequently retain the old whodunit element, with a degree of characterisation and social commentary found in too few novels of the more classical form.

Dashiell Hammett (1894–1961) was the undisputed father of the school. It would be wrong to regard his work as sheer sensationalism, or even to categorise his books purely as hard boiled. Although his detectives display a toughness and cynicism which was revolutionary, they are also capable of compassion and have an inherent honesty; very few of Hammett's imitators have been able to produce characters with quite the same strength of personality. It is Hammett's dialogue which makes his novels memorable, and he has been seriously compared with both Faulkner and Hemingway in this respect. In

HAMMETT Dashiell
The Maltese falcon
New York Knopf 1930; Cassell 1931

Sam Spade, the prototype of the private eye which has hardly ever been bettered by subsequent authors, elbows and wisecracks his way in pursuit of the person who killed his partner. There can be few readers – particularly in view of the excellent film version starring Bogart – who do not know that the root of all the evil is a priceless black falcon statuette. But the book, on rereading, still impresses with its pace, its crisp dialogue, and the sting in the tail. If this is Hammett's most famous book, it is generally accepted that

HAMMETT Dashiell
The glass key
New York Knopf 1931; Cassell 1933

is his best. It represented his full development as a novelist, not just as a crime writer but an explorer of human relationships. The most important is that between Ned Beaumont, the intelligent 'fixer' working in the ruthless milieu of political chicanery, and his boss Paul Madvig.

It is more, far more, than the story of Beaumont's search for the killer of a New York senator's son. The world of gambling, of gangsters, of politics, is all here in a manner which suggests most vividly that guilt and innocence are relative terms and there is often a thin dividing line. What a pity it is that Hammett is judged too frequently as a crime writer, a pulp writer even, when voices in the wilderness have compared him with some of the finest American novelists.

A contemporary of Hammett, James M Cain produced a novel with an intriguing title,

CAIN James M
The postman always rings twice
New York Knopf 1934; Cape 1934

which is a comparatively slight volume with a well worn theme – the wife and lover who plan to eliminate the husband. It has been done before and since, but this particular book stands out for its economy of words, and the rough justice of its denouement which makes the reader's sympathy difficult to place. It is a portrayal of two amateur murderers enmeshed in a situation where they cannot escape from each other, prisoners alternately of love and of the consequences of their act. It may be a reviewer's cliché to read a book 'at a sitting', but this one should be devoured whole for the full effect.

Raymond Chandler (1888–1959) has been mentioned already, but he ranks with Hammett as the quintessence of the hard boiled school. Although his work might seem as American as his birth, Chandler was brought up and educated in England. His experience of life was considerable, as he passed through many occupations before becoming a contributor to pulp magazines. To his later writing he brought a worldly manner and a degree of shrewd observation which justified his own contention that a plot should not be regarded as more important than the actual writing. He set out to write well, and succeeded admirably. His way with words, his characterisation and his almost exceptional gift for dialogue improved markedly as his output increased. The few novels featuring Philip Marlowe, the private investigator who could cut someone down to size with a wisecrack, are of course the basis of Chandler's fine reputation in the field.

Marlowe is a good guy, but not embarrassingly so; an honourable man, if this isn't old hat, who abhors cruelty and corruption. There is very little to choose between the Marlowe novels, although

CHANDLER Raymond
The high window
New York Knopf 1942; Hamish Hamilton 1943

is outstanding. It concerns the theft of a rare coin, followed by two murders, and contains richly assorted characters nice, neurotic and nasty. It is a whodunit without the vicarage tea party atmosphere, and its principal players are of flesh and blood. This is where Chandler succeeded whereas so many of his later imitators failed.

Although regarded as a follower of Hammett and very much a representative of the hard boiled school, Jonathan Latimer demonstrates a degree of lightheartedness, sometimes combined with more sexual explicitness than many writers of the period displayed. There is very little situation comedy in his novels – he left this to others such as Elliot Paul and Craig Rice – but the dialogue is liberally laced with humour. In

LATIMER Jonathan
The lady in the morgue
New York Doubleday-Doran 1936; Methuen 1937

private detective Bill Crane, although less physical than some of Hammett's creations, is still the master of the wisecrack. This is no mean tribute to Jonathan Latimer's skill; so many later writers tried their hands at it, and either failed miserably or descended to the level of unintentional pastiche. Crane, on this occasion, is faced with the problem of a corpse which is stolen from the morgue, and the murder of an attendant. The action is fast and furious.

'From the way her buttocks looked under the black silk dress, I knew she'd be good in bed.' These opening words by private detective Karl Craven give a foretaste of what some critics regard as Latimer's best novel,

LATIMER Jonathan
Solomon's vineyard
Methuen 1941

It is an advance on *The lady in the morgue*; less humour, more violence, and considerably more sex, including a masochistic broad. Nevertheless it is unlikely to arouse the disgust of the reader, as do many present day writers who cover the same subjects with markedly inferior literary ability. Latimer also brings to this story a theme previously used by Hammett – who killed the detective's partner? – and a novel idea connecting gangsters with a rather questionable religious sect.

Another follower in the wake of Hammett was Cornell Woolrich (1903–1968), who wrote also as 'William Irish'.

WOOLRICH Cornell
The bride wore black
New York Simon & Schuster 1940; Robert Hale 1942

is a taut tale of an unknown woman who enters the lives of four men, strikes, and then disappears. Who was this beautiful murderess, and what was her motive? A fifth man is next on the list, and the reader is left in some doubt until the final pages as to whether the killer will succeed again. It builds to an exciting climax. Woolrich's technique was based upon subordinating everything to what he called the 'line of suspense'. Irrespective of one's acceptance or otherwise of the technical term, it certainly worked. It can be seen again under his *alter ego* in

IRISH William
Phantom lady
Philadelphia Lippincott 1942; Robert Hale 1945

which shows a young man. Scott Henderson, in a predicament. At the time his wife is being strangled with his necktie, he is wining and dining a mysterious lady. So mysterious is she, in fact, that no-one else can remember having seen her or can vouch for her existence – which is distinctly awkward for Scott, who is convicted of murder and sentenced to the electric chair. The dialogue crackles, and the pace moves fast toward the day of execution.

In spite of various excellent examples, many of the writers who followed Hammett and Chandler in style are little known today. Take, for example, 'Wade Miller'. This was a pseudonym adopted by two ex-sergeants of the US Army when they collaborated to write crime novels. Bob Wade and Bill Miller wrote a dozen or so novels under this name, and others under the name 'Whit Masterson', and of these

MILLER Wade
Deadly weapon
New York Farrar, Straus 1946; Sampson Low, Marston 1947

was the first and received great acclaim. It contains several well drawn characters, notably the detective Walter James, stripper Shasta Lynn, and a dry cop named Austin Clapp. The plot has the pace and violence of Hammett, without his inherent commentary upon the corruption which he sees around. It also has a sensational climax, and among a mass of similar books it calls out for greater recognition.

A hard boiled novel without a detective, in the tradition of Cain rather than Hammett, was written by Eleazar Lipsky and aptly entitled

LIPSKY Eleazar
The kiss of death
New York Penguin 1947; Penguin 1949

Vanni Bianco is a hardened criminal; his environment, and the fact that as a boy he saw his father gunned down by a cop, has made sure of it. To him crime is a normal way of life, and the police informer is the lowest of the low. This short novel shows how Bianco, even though he retains the highest code of honour, becomes an informer himself. The Assistant District Attorney, with his symbol of the open door to a happy family existence, leaves Bianco little choice. But for a man with such a record, finding himself between two camps, there can be no real freedom. This is an exciting story of hard men, and yet one of the saddest crime novels one is likely to come across.

Like Lipsky's novel, that of William Wiegand is not as well known as it deserves to be. The central character of

WIEGAND William
At last, Mr Tolliver
New York Rinehart 1950; Hodder and Stoughton 1951

is an elderly and discredited ex-doctor who lives in a seedy boarding house. Once a doctor to hoodlums, he is no longer practising but ekes out an existence in a shop selling stamps and coins. He has a dream, the only thing which means anything to him – to carry out medical work in Brazil, and to set up a laboratory there. When one of his fellow boarders is murdered and suspicion falls upon everyone in the house, it is likely that the boorish Lieutenant Carmichael will unearth Tolliver's past, and the old man's dream looks less and less like becoming a reality. So Tolliver himself begins to investigate the murder, to use his knowledge of the underworld to expose the killer. But behind him all the time is Carmichael. The figure of the unscrupulous Carmichael and the sympathetically portrayed Tolliver combine to make this a memorable book. It has a harshness, and yet at the same time a tenderness which few American crime novels display.

8 Towards modern crime fiction

Dashiell Hammett's best work appeared in 1930–1931. It actually co-incided with another refreshing deviation from conventional detective themes which was given life by Anthony Berkeley in England. He had already flouted the rules or sailed close to the wind in several of his novels, two of which were cited earlier. It was in his books as 'Francis Iles', however, that his ideas reached full development. The first was

> ILES Francis
> Malice aforethought. The story of a commonplace crime
> Victor Gollancz 1931

and this was followed by

> ILES Francis
> Before the fact. A murder story for ladies
> Victor Gollancz 1932

'It was not until several weeks after he had decided to murder his wife that Dr Bickleigh took any active steps in the matter.' 'Some women give birth to murderers, some go to bed with them, and some marry them. Lina Aysgarth had lived with her husband for nearly eight years before she realised that she was married to a murderer.'

These are the opening sentences respectively of the first two Iles titles, and significantly indicate that they presented something entirely different in the world of detective fiction. The mind of the murderer was established as more important than his identity, and indeed his identity was revealed on the first page rather than the last. Although Iles was not the first to use the technique, these two novels provided the inspiration for a whole new school of crime fiction exemplified by many present day writers.

In both books we are made to feel that murder is not a sensational subject, in fact it is planned in the cosy drawing rooms of English suburbia just as painstakingly as in the dens of the criminal classes. The examination of the murder's mind, and the gradual revelation of how he proceeds with his plan, makes the Iles technique just as enthralling as a detective novel in the classic mould. The element of surprise regarding the murderer's identity has been replaced by the questions: will the murderer carry out his plan, and will he get away with it? But this would be too simplistic a definition of the Iles methods, as he shows that there are more ways of springing surprises than even the most seasoned reader will appreciate.

The crime novel which poses questions other than 'whodunit?' is very much a phenomenon of the past thirty years, and is much in evidence today. Although many of the authors owe much to Francis Iles, he was himself anticipated by a much earlier book by R Austin Freeman, at least insomuch that Freeman made the first significant attempt to break away from the conventional puzzle format.

Freeman was in any case something of an innovator, in that Dr Thorndyke employed scientific methods in the detection of crime far more than any other detective, including Holmes, had done previously. Freeman actually went so far as to experiment with many of his techniques in his own laboratory. His principal innovation, however, was the creation of the 'inverted' detective story, the first examples of which are collected in

FREEMAN R Austin
The singing bone
Hodder & Stoughton 1912

Freeman asked himself, to quote from the preface, 'Would it be possible to write a detective story in which, from the outset, the reader was taken entirely into the author's confidence, was made an actual witness of the crime and furnished with every fact that could possibly be used in its detection? Would there be any story left to tell when the reader had all these facts?' He was convinced that the idea would be successful, and was proved correct. Indeed it established a type of detective story which later became fully accepted. The idea was to be improved upon, and to be elaborated in various directions, by many writers whose works will be quoted in this section.

The element of surprise, and of the reader being caught unawares by a clever detective, is of course absent. But the reader is compensated by being in a position of superiority, of knowing all the facts before the detective is even called in, and a different kind of satisfaction is derived from observing the detective at work. The question is 'how will the detective prove the criminal's guilt?' rather than 'whodunit?'

In her introduction to *Great short stories of detection, mystery and horror* (Victor Gollancz 1928) Dorothy L Sayers remarked that 'Mr Freeman has had few followers, and appears to have himself abandoned the formula, which is rather a pity.' It was not until later that

Freeman's idea was to bear fruit in the work of other writers who succeeded in establishing the 'inverted' detective story as something far more than an intriguing experiment.

Another precursor of the modern crime novel is

LOWNDES Marie Belloc
The lodger
Methuen 1913

which was inspired by the Ripper murders of the late 1880s, and Mrs Belloc Lowndes (1868-1947) makes a reasonably competent job of conveying the terror which existed in London while the unknown killer stalked the streets. Mr and Mrs Bunting have a new lodger, Mr Sleuth, and from the outset there is something not quite right about him. Clearly he is a gentleman fallen upon hard times to rent such modest lodgings, although he has money for rent in advance. But he turns all the pictures with their faces to the wall, and behaves in other odd ways which gradually begin to prey upon Mrs Bunting's mind. Is he the Avenger, the maniacal killer whose sobriquet is on the lips of every Londoner?

Critics are divided as to whether or not this famous work by Mrs Belloc Lowndes bears any comparison with the Iles school. Certainly there can be no argument about another pre-Iles novel, written by C S Forester (1899–1966). Not only pre-Iles but also pre-Hornblower,

FORESTER C S
Payment deferred
John Lane 1926

is cast very much in the mould of Iles. Mr Marble, an impecunious bank clerk, finds it increasingly difficult to support his family in their modest South London house, and sees the ideal opportunity to pay off his debts when a wealthy nephew arrives from Australia. The visitor is young and alone in the world, and murder occurs surprisingly naturally in this commonplace setting of suburban normality. Mr Marble, having murdered, finds himself being dragged further into the mire together with his family, and the denouement is shattering.

Richard Henry Sampson (1896–1973), using the name 'Richard Hull', wrote a dozen or so crime novels in the wake of Francis Iles, the first and best of which is

HULL Richard
The murder of my aunt
Faber & Faber 1934

Hull made no secret of the fact that he was so impressed by the technique of Iles that he set out to follow the same course. He wrote in the first person, and this was no doubt to enhance the reader's appreciation of the motives and mind of the murderer. Some of his narrators have far from cosy minds. Their intentions are more frequently the sort of deliberate and coldblooded murder with which the reader can not sympathise, rather than the elimination of someone whose demise would be a distinct gain to society. The aunt in the first title is not everyone's favourite type, but we nonetheless find difficulty in associating with nephew Edward, who plans to murder her. As with Iles, the interest lies in observing the potential murderer's plans step by step, proceeding at a quite leisurely pace until we are stopped in our tracks by the neat twist at the end.

The short detective stories of F Tennyson Jesse (1889–1958) featuring the extrasensory Solange Fontaine are not remembered today. Her reputation rests mainly upon

JESSE F Tennyson
A pin to see the peepshow
William Heinemann 1934

and a recent television adaptation brought renewed interest in this excellent novel. It bears the stamp of documentary fiction, being soundly based upon the Thompson and Bywaters murder case. Julia Almond, who is Miss Jesse's reincarnation of Edith Thompson, is portrayed as a girl of sheltered upbringing and romantic inclinations. Her marriage to an older man is unsuccessful, and her affair with the young Leonard Carr leads to flights of fantasy which seem inevitably to result in murder. The Thompson and Bywaters case was a *cause célèbre* which shook England, and here the reconstruction follows the same pattern as the real life trial, the verdict and the shocking conclusion.

The infallibility of the British legal system was scarcely ever questioned by the writers of pure detective novels; the guilty rarely went free, and the innocent were never hanged. When the modern crime novel began to emerge in the 1930s, however, the reader was frequently left to draw his own conclusions – as in this case.

The renowned wine expert Raymond Postgate (1896–1971) wrote several detective novels. The one which particularly stands out as following the trend against the accepted classic form is

POSTGATE Raymond
Verdict of twelve

Collins 1940

which will probably survive as one of the unique examples of the genre. There have been others which use the courtroom as a setting but none quite in this way. The case concerns the murder of a small boy, who dies of poisoning. His aunt is put on trial, and we see the case from the standpoint of each member of the jury. The character of each juror is sketched by means of the flashback, and we begin to see why each individual juror might interpret the evidence in his or her own peculiar way. As the trial proceeds, and the time draws nearer when the life of the accused will be literally in the hands of these twelve people, the drama of the situation is more skilfully conveyed than in most other courtroom novels.

A particularly fine and realistic crime novel is

HAMILTON Patrick
Hangover Square; or, the man with two minds. A story of darkest Earl's Court in the year 1939
Constable 1941

which explores the mind of a man driven to murder. Patrick Hamilton (1904–1962) wrote such evergreen stage melodramas as *Rope* and *Gaslight*, and here he brilliantly conveys the atmosphere of 'darkest Earl's Court' and draws with sympathy and consummate skill the feckless members of the gang with which the unfortunate George Harvey Bone becomes involved. As a novel of London, and as a horrifying picture of a man's decline, this must surely be a prime example of the sort of book which has shaken the world of crime fiction out of its pre-war cosiness.

'Shelley Smith', real name Nancy Bodington, is another writer in the tradition inspired by Francis Iles, although she adds her own deft touch of icy menace. Characterisation and criminal psychology replace the puzzle element – although, as with Iles, the surprising twists and turns of the plot are more than sufficient compensation for the loss of the whodunit flavour. *The Lord have mercy* (Hamish Hamilton 1956; still in print) was highly praised, but

SMITH Shelley
Come and be killed
Collins 1946

is selected here as the best of the early examples of Shelley Smith's promise. It tells of Florence Brown, a markedly neurotic spinster, who enters a nursing home following a suicide attempt. When she discharges herself from the home, it becomes a clear case of 'out of the frying pan . . .' For she meets the plump and motherly Mrs Jolly, and Mrs Jolly is a murderess.

The unusual central idea employed by Kenneth Fearing (1902–1961) in

FEARING Kenneth
The big clock
New York Harcourt, Brace 1946; Bodley Head 1947

has gained it a permanent place among the great crime novels. It was adapted into an extremely successful film starring Charles Laughton. Earl Janoth, a rich and unspeakable magazine proprietor, kills his mistress and then discovers that someone saw him go to her apartment just before the murder. He employs one of his staff, George Stroud, to find the witness – which happens to be Stroud himself. The predicament of appearing to carry out a search for oneself, yet striving deliberately to fail, is well thought out and skilfully portrayed. Stroud realises, however, that Janoth's vast resources will ensure that his identity as the witness will inevitably be revealed. Naturally he fears the consequences, and this makes an enthralling crime novel of considerable pace.

At this point, having quoted the most notable predecessors and successors of Francis Iles, it might be useful to define some of the factors inherent in the modern crime novel as compared with the classical form. Basically it is important to realise that whereas the pure detective story asks 'who?' and sometimes little else, the modern crime novel allows 'why?' and 'how?' to assume greater significance. There are other basic differences, and an excellent tabulation appears in chapter fourteen of Julian Symons' *Bloody murder* (Faber 1972; Penguin 1974).

It must be appreciated that the modern crime novel is a hybrid. It is not easy to generalise. Some show crime at its most violent, others are as cosy as their predecessors of the twenties. Again it must be emphasised that the identity of the criminal is not *always* revealed at the outset – in fact in some cases it is not revealed at all! The tracking down of the criminal is seen sometimes from the viewpoint of the pursuer, sometimes from that of the pursued. There is clear interest in criminal psychology; in the little man or woman involuntarily drawn out of their depth into a criminal situation from which there is no escape; and in the humdrum, everyday scene where an ordinary person is driven to uncharacteristic violence.

A forced generalisation, however, would draw attention to the modern crime novel's interest in the cause of a crime, to its characterisation as opposed to the often cardboard figures of detective fiction, and above all to its status as a novel worthy of more serious consideration than critics have hitherto displayed.

One of the most interesting features of the modern crime novel is that it is prepared to question police methods. The policemen of John Bingham and John Wainwright, among other authors who are quoted later, are by no means the shining lights which some other writers make them out to be.

Some authors even prick the bubble of infallibility which surrounds the British legal system. One of the earliest to do so was Edgar Lustgarten, who perhaps significantly has made a study of the subject over many years. He has established a reputation as a skilled commentator on criminal trials and the machinery of justice. His work has been presented in almost every medium. Understandably, therefore, he has brought to his handful of crime novels a unique knowledge, and

LUSTGARTEN Edgar
A case to answer
Eyre & Spottiswoode 1947

is a thought provoking example. A Soho prostitute is murdered and mutilated, and a man is placed on trial. He is a respectable family man, holding a good position with a reputable city firm, yet he was connected with the dead woman and the police have evidence against him. Edgar Lustgarten takes us through the trial, and we see it from the standpoint of the police, the witnesses, the judge and counsel. The verdict is finally reached, but there is more to come.

The complete master of the 'inverted' detective short story, as originated by R Austin Freeman, was Roy Vickers (1889–1965). In the collection

VICKERS Roy
The Department of Dead Ends
Faber & Faber 1949

we know the murderer from the outset, we see his motive and the workings of his mind, and we observe the crime being committed. The surprise element is embodied in the question – how will the police crack the case? The Department of Dead Ends at Scotland Yard contains the files of unsolved cases, together with clues and objects which have not been hitherto fitted into their places in the respective jigsaws. Inspector Rason, sometimes many years after the event, has the job of connecting the unconnected and breaking the unbreakable alibi. Normally it is a small everyday object – be it a yellow jumper or a baby's trumpet – which brings the murderer to book, and this adds to the stories a fascination and realism all their own. There is, too, an element of sadness without sentimentality, most of the murderers being ordinary citizens rather than vicious killers. Even the staunchest advocate of capital punishment should finish these stories with a feeling of sympathy and compassion. A further volume of excellent stories appeared as

VICKERS Roy
Murder will out: Nine Dead Ends stories
Faber and Faber 1950

Although Vickers' mastery of the 'inverted' technique is unquestioned, it had in fact been used slightly earlier by an old hand, Freeman Wills Crofts. In his collection of twenty three short stories entitled

CROFTS Freeman Wills
Murderers make mistakes
Hodder & Stoughton 1947

there are twelve in which the criminal's actions are first described, and then Chief Inspector French reveals how he learnt the truth.

Very far removed from the classic detective story, but aligned with the contributions of Iles and Lustgarten, is

GRIERSON Edward
Reputation for a song
Chatto & Windus 1952

which is at once a competent study of a domestic murder and a fine example of courtroom drama. Robert Anderson is a stolid and respectable solicitor in a small town, and his family problems are not untypical. It is his son Rupert, however, whose contempt for his father develops into a rankling hatred which culminates in murder. The narrative builds up skilfully towards the crime, after which we witness the attempts of various members of the family to secure Rupert's acquittal. Their ends can only be achieved by blackening the reputation of the deceased, to impress upon the jury that the case is one of self defence rather than premeditated murder. A domestic tragedy, a trial drama with the verdict on the final page; either way it is a perfect example of the new direction in crime writing.

The first and decidedly best book by 'John Bingham', the family name of Lord Clanmorris, is

BINGHAM John

My name is Michael Sibley
Victor Gollancz 1952
in which the author attempts realism in his portrayal of police officers.
It is frightening, to say the least, although one might feel that Michael
Sibley has only himself to blame in his gruelling encounter with the
law. His friend Prosset has been murdered, and he is himself under
suspicion, but his attempts to extricate himself are gradually revealed
as lies and subterfuge. The police are convinced of his guilt, and subject him to a series of harrowing interviews. We follow his various
changes of mind, and know his innermost feelings, in this first person
narration of a man who is innocent but feels the weight of the law
bearing down upon him.

From the police of Bingham, British or perhaps unBritish, we turn
to the thoroughly American cops of
WAUGH Hillary
Last seen wearing. . .
New York Doubleday 1952; Victor Gollancz 1953
who are concerned with the sudden disappearance of eighteen year
old Marilyn Lowell Mitchell from her college in Massachusetts. We
are treated to a gritty and sharply authentic narrative of step-by-step
police investigation in the American style. The police novels which
have come out of the USA, with a few exceptions like the work of Hillary Waugh and Ed McBain, are either excessively brutal or artificially contrived. Waugh has succeeded in producing small town
police tales which can rouse the reader's excitement by their very
meticulousness, by the very dullness which is ninety per cent of any
investigation. Although he has never excelled this particular novel for
sheer originality, Waugh's other work is all of exceptionally high standard.

A further example of the solid modern novel of police procedure
comes from perhaps a surprising source – that underrated writer John
Creasey (1908–1973). As is well known, Creasey used a number of
pseudonyms and produced a long list of thrillers which made him
probably the most successful writer in the field since Edgar Wallace.
Indeed his work resembles that of Wallace in many ways – the economy of style, fast action, plenty of dialogue, and almost total lack of
characterisation. Most of his books, like those of Wallace, come
within the field of the action thriller rather than detective fiction. In
1955, however, he made a major breakthrough under the name 'J J
Marric' when he created the character George Gideon. In the first

book of what was to become a phenomenally popular series,

MARRIC J J
Gideon's day
Hodder & Stoughton 1955

Gideon holds the rank of Detective Superintendent at New Scotland Yard. He is a dependable character of greater credibility than Creasey's other heroes, and was to develop in stature and in rank as later novels appeared. The Gideon novels stand out as approaching the documentary. Gideon's working day involves him in dope peddling, robbery, murder and gang violence. The style was at the time something new, as the story switches from one case to another until finally the loose ends are tied up. This presents a complex picture of the life of a busy detective, and strikes one as all the more realistic for that.

Gideon's day, together with *Gideon's week* (Hodder & Stoughton 1956) and *Gideon's night* (Hodder & Stoughton 1957) comprise

MARRIC J J
The Gideon omnibus
Hodder & Stoughton 1964

Probably the best known team of cops, however, is that created by Evan Hunter under the pseudonym 'Ed McBain'. The 87th precinct novels have during the past twenty years extended into a series of a uniformly high standard. Two early examples,

McBAIN Ed
Cop hater
New York Simon & Schuster 1956; T V Boardman 1958

and

McBAIN Ed
The mugger
New York Simon & Schuster 1956; T V Boardman 1959

were followed by many others which were well received on both sides of the Atlantic. The attraction of the 87th precinct novels lies in the author's versatility, and in his successful compromise between the dull routine of detective work and the incredible sensationalism displayed by so many other writers. His versatility is clearly seen; the books display violence on some occasions, almost knockabout comedy on others. The characters are conveyed brutally or sympathetically as the situation demands. We see the detectives as human beings with private lives, as fallible beings with loves and hates and the almost impossible onus to remain impartial. New York, with its violent crime, provides ample employment for the men of the 87th precinct, and each of McBain's novels shows them coping with an interrelated set of cases.

The Swiss writer Friedrich Dürrenmatt also makes use of police detectives, but his books can not be described as police novels in the same way that one would apply the term to McBain or Marric. And of course they are a mile away from the realistic narratives of, say, Maurice Procter. In Dürrenmatt's case the policeman is used as a symbol, as a means of ensuring that everything is subordinated to the ends of justice. In his most widely quoted book

DÜRRENMATT Friedrich
> The judge and his hangman: Translated from the German by Cyrus Brooks
> Herbert Jenkins 1954

Inspector Barlach, old and ill, works toward the final confrontation with the monstrous criminal to whose downfall the detective's whole career has been dedicated. But Barlach is no Superintendent Gideon and he does not operate according to the book. His own life is running out, and the normal processes of law can not be relied upon to give him the ultimate satisfaction of a lifetime's work. Dürrenmatt's skill at building suspense, his mastery of the bizarre situation, and his use of the classical surprise denouement, are however all subordinated to the force of his moral argument that evil must be punished by any possible means. In this case Barlach, officially investigating the murder of a young police officer, feels that he can serve the ends of justice only by appointing himself judge – and by planning an execution.

An intriguing writer with several good novels to her credit is Margot Bennett, who was in top form in

BENNETT Margot
> The man who didn't fly
> Eyre & Spottiswoode 1955

Four men propose to fly to Dublin, but only three of them are on the plane when it crashes. Who and where is the fourth, and why did he disappear? It is necessary to delve into the past life of the four in order to fit the pieces of the puzzle together, and it is here that Miss Bennett scores with her perceptive drawing of people. There is even a mystery to be solved in the true deductive manner. Although less conventional than her earlier works, this novel displays the full range of Margot Bennett's wit, ingenuity, and command of dialogue.

The works of Nicholas Blake were mostly in the classic form, and several were quoted in section 6. On a few occasions, however, he produced work outside the whodunit format and demonstrated what a really superlative novelist he was.

BLAKE Nicholas
A tangled web
Collins 1956

is not typical of his work, but it was one of his own favourites and is by any standards an excellent book. Based on an Edwardian *cause célèbre*, it concerns the love of a simple girl for a young cat-burglar with the charm of Raffles. The murder of a policeman puts their love to the test, and the author depicts the investigating officers determined to run their quarry to ground. A story of poignant love, and of despicable betrayal, it is also beautifully written.

Both *The beast must die* and *A tangled web* are included in *The Nicholas Blake omnibus* (Collins 1966), with an introduction by the author, and together with another brilliant study in premeditated murder, *A penknife in my heart* (Collins 1958).

How can one describe the works of Patricia Highsmith? Rather artificially classified, they would come under the umbrella of the psychological thriller. But they do not set out to thrill. On the contrary, there is a 'there but for the grace of God. . .' quality about them which makes them frankly disturbing.

HIGHSMITH Patricia
The blunderer
New York Coward-McCann 1954; Cresset Press 1956

is typical, and is arguably her best. Its central character is a young lawyer, Walter Stackhouse, who would dearly like to be rid of his wife – and in this case many readers would not blame him. Could he, he wonders, copy a murder recently committed by another man? From the moment his mind turns to thoughts of murder, he begins to sink deeper into a chasm from which there is no escape. Lieutenant Lawrence Corby is determined to obtain confessions from both men, and has no qualms about the methods he employs. He plays them one against the other, with tragic and appalling results.

There is rather more of the puzzle element in the works of Pierre Boileau and Thomas Narcejac, whose books are normally labelled 'Boileau-Narcejac'. Although they normally present a mystery, and the atmosphere of suspense is built up until a surprise denouement, they are still far from the classical approach. There is no systematic investigation, sifting of evidence, and so on. Instead the Boileau-Narcejac novels demonstrate a mixture of human relationships, with a crime and a detective of some sort who becomes personally more than professionally involved. Their best work is

BOILEAU-NARCEJAC
The living and the dead: Translated by Geoffrey Sainsbury
Hutchinson 1956

which was adapted as the Hitchcock film *Vertigo*. It starts apparently simply, with a man hiring a detective to watch his wife, whom he believes to be suicidal. But the complications of the plot, and the ingenuity of the book when all is revealed, mark Boileau-Narcejac as one (or two) of the few consistently good crime writers to have been translated from the French.

The exploration of criminal psychology is even more fascinating when inspired by real life crime, and one example which will remain a cornerstone of the genre is

LEVIN Meyer
Compulsion
New York Simon & Schuster 1956; Frederick Muller 1957

a major novel which became a memorable film. This is one of the few attempts to explore the mind of the motiveless murderer. It is based upon the celebrated Loeb and Leopold case of 1924. Two Chicago students, both of wealthy families and above average intelligence, decide to commit the perfect crime. The kidnapping and murder of a millionaire's son is that crime, and we follow the story step by step; the murder, the trial, the verdict. It is a long novel, shocking but positively stimulating. The attitude of many readers to the case, as with its real life counterpart, will be that such bestial murderers ought to be put down like mad dogs. Meyer Levin psychoanalyses, however, rather than merely presenting a crime documentary. 'I do not follow the aphorism that to understand all is to forgive all,' he says in his foreword. 'But surely we all believe in healing, more than in punishment.'

The work of Julian Symons as a historian and critic in the field of crime fiction is well known. In journal articles, and of course in his invaluable book *Bloody murder* (Faber 1972; Penguin 1974), he traces the development from detective story to crime novel. His own books have followed this pattern. After some competent detective stories in the classical tradition, which were but examples of a very large field, he turned to the crime novel. The 'why?' and the 'how?' began to assume greater significance in his books than the 'who?', although the latter sometimes remained a factor. In some cases the identity of the murderer still remains doubtful at the end of the book, and this apparent failure to tie up neatly all loose ends is a marked difference between the detective story and the crime novel.

The first book which showed Symons' transition to the full, and received critical acclaim from the Crime Writers' Association as the best crime novel of its year, was

SYMONS Julian
The colour of murder
Collins 1957

The book is divided into two parts. In the first, John Wilkins' statement to a consultant psychiatrist, we see a picture of an unexceptional suburban husband with a bitchy wife. Wilkins strikes up a relationship with an assistant in his local library, and begins to create around her a world of fantasy in which his wife has little part. He is a frustrated man, and also suffers from blackouts. It is almost inevitable that murder occurs to create the break in the triangle, although events do not perhaps develop in the way the reader expects. The second part of the book, in which Wilkins faces trial for murder, is enthralling and displays the author's ability to communicate the courtroom atmosphere which his subsequent books were to confirm and improve upon. The outcome of the case is – well, suffice it to say that it marks the difference between the detective story and the crime novel.

There are not many contemporary writers who can produce a genuinely absorbing *roman policier*. Symons can and consistently does, a noteworthy example being

SYMONS Julian
The progress of a crime
Collins 1960

On Guy Fawkes night, around the bonfire on the village green, there are unwelcome intruders – motorcycle thugs from the city. When the motorcycles leave, a man lies stabbed to death. From this point develops a painstaking investigation and murder trial, throughout which the author provides thumbnail sketches of a host of journalists, police, and characters savoury and unsavoury. The central character, a journalist following the best story of his career, finds it impossible not to become emotionally involved. The reader too, as with most of Julian Symons' work, will not be able to bestow his sympathies or condemnation lightly, realising that in this imperfect world it is not always a question simply of right or wrong.

One more example will serve to demonstrate Symons' craftsmanship – dare one say supremacy? – in the field of the contemporary crime novel in England. In

SYMONS Julian
The end of Solomon Grundy
Collins 1964

a 'model' (say no more) is murdered in a London mews flat. The trail leads to a suburban housing estate called The Dell, populated by various members of the middle class – and Solomon Grundy. Grundy is a misfit in The Dell, almost if not more than his coloured neighbour Mr Kabanga. It soon becomes obvious that the police regard Grundy as their prime suspect, and many of his so-called friends and Dell dwellers can well believe it. After all, what better reasons than his irascibility and failure to conform? As a piece of social commentary it is first class. As a courtroom drama, with Symons regulars Eustace Hardy and Magnus Newton, it is riveting. But as a question – what *was* the end of Solomon Grundy? – it will long remain in the reader's mind.

The progress of a crime and *The end of Solomon Grundy* are included in *The Julian Symons omnibus* (Collins 1967; still in print), with an introduction by the author, and together with the earlier *The thirty-first of February* (Victor Gollancz 1950).

9 The state of the art

The world of crime fiction in the sixties and seventies has presented a mixture of the various forms which have been discussed in the earlier sections. To date no dominant form has emerged, and in spite of some prophecies of doom the classic type of detective novel remains with us. It is true, however, that an increasing number of crime novels without the puzzle element has appeared during the past twenty years or so.

Various authors of the sixties and seventies can be quoted as evidence of the continued popularity of the classic formula, and it has also been evident that new writers were still emerging who will be able to evolve a few novel twists and to present detectives of originality.

The solid and dependable police detective, for example, was still to be seen in the works of Alan Hunter and Gil North. Hunter's thoughtful Chief Superintendent Gently, who in his own way is a philosopher as well as a razor-sharp detective, first appeared in

> HUNTER Alan
> Gently does it
> Cassell 1955

and impressed readers with his patience and his tolerance, as well as his dogged persistence. Characterisation is sound in the Gently novels, and few patently cardboard creations appear in these well written works. A good introduction is

> HUNTER Alan
> Gently in an omnibus
> Cassell 1966

which consists of: *Gently does it; Gently through the mill* (Cassell 1958); and *Gently in the sun* (Cassell 1959)

Gil North's contribution to the list of great detectives is Sergeant Caleb Cluff, who has appeared in a long series of novels beginning with

> NORTH Gil
> Sergeant Cluff stands firm
> Chapman and Hall 1960

and has been the subject of a popular television series. Cluff is obstinate but wholly likeable, with a love of the Yorkshire countryside matched only by his love for his fellow man. Sentimental it most certainly is not, for Cluff is motivated to right wrongs rather than to demand retribution. He knows everyone in Gunnarshaw, and they know him. His methods work, although sometimes Inspector Mole might disapprove.

Another original detective and an unusual setting were devised by John and Felicity Coulson, who wrote a highly competent series of detective novels in the classic form, using the pseudonym 'John and Emery Bonett'. Some were set in Spain and feature the courteous and unassuming Inspector Borges. One of the best,

BONETT John and Emery
This side murder?
Michael Joseph 1967

concerns the murder of the unpopular Gilbert Tarsier, a newspaper columnist who is a distinct embarrassment to the guests at the luxury hotel in Cala Cristina. A tissue of lies, evasions and self protection has to be pierced by Borges before he reaches the solution. One of the novel features – a complete recipe for *paella Catalana* – adds a brilliant touch of authenticity.

The sobriquet 'queen of crime', which was used earlier to describe Agatha Christie among others, is not likely to die while new authors such as Patricia Moyes and Emma Lathen are emerging. Miss Moyes, with her series detective Chief Superintendent Henry Tibbett, has devised some ingenious plots. In particular

MOYES Patricia
Who saw her die?
Collins 1970

is a piece of classic detection of the good old school. The house party murder with suspects galore might be old hat, but the author scores with her highly original murder methods. Critics have gone so far as to compare her with Christie and Sayers.

Patricia Moyes is also adept at ringing the changes as far as her backgrounds are concerned, and

MOYES Patricia
Season of snows and sins
Collins 1971

finds Tibbett on holiday in a Swiss ski resort. Each year the departure of the international set leaves a host of problems for the locals at the end of the season. This year it would appear to be a *crime passionel*, but Tibbett thinks otherwise.

'Emma Lathen', who is in fact Mary Latis and Martha Hennissart, writes conventional detective novels with a financial background. John Putnam Thatcher of the Sloan Guaranty Trust in New York is the series detective. Some of the novels have a Wall Street setting, while others show Thatcher against different backgrounds which nevertheless have connections with his firm. They are well written and uniformly competent with just sufficient humour, and probably a good introduction to this excellent series is

> LATHEN Emma
> Banking on death
> New York Macmillan 1961; Victor Gollancz 1962

together with

> LATHEN Emma
> Accounting for murder
> New York Macmillan 1964; Victor Gollancz 1965

which tells of the murder of a man who has been agitating for an enquiry into the affairs of a large firm.

Particular mention for original detectives of the sixties and seventies, however, must be made of Harry Kemelman and John Ball in America, and James McClure in Britain.

Kemelman's detective has been described as America's answer to Father Brown, although there is little doubt that the creation of such a figure was not his foremost intention. He set out to write novels of the Jewish suburban community, and found that the rabbi's accepted function as a judge and as a legal interpreter placed this central figure in an ideal position to play detective. Thus Rabbi David Small was born, and he appeared in a successful series of detective novels beginning with

> KEMELMAN Harry
> Friday the rabbi slept late
> New York Crown 1964; Hutchinson 1965

Kemelman also showed his skill in short stories, and proved to be one of the few modern exponents of pure armchair detection. Previously published in *Ellery Queen's mystery magazine*, the stories contained in

> KEMELMAN Harry
> The nine mile walk: The Nicky Welt stories
> New York Putnam 1967; Hutchinson 1968

are models of the art. In an introduction the author explains how they came to be written, and a little of his philosophy of the detective story.

Nicky Welt is a professor of English language and literature, and the storyteller is a modern 'Watson' who dines or plays chess with Welt while marvelling at his reasoned solutions to the latest murders.

John Ball's detective, Virgil Tibbs, is original because he is black. Virgil's first appearance in

BALL John
In the heat of the night
New York Harper & Row 1965; Michael Joseph 1966

sees him in the distinctly unfriendly surroundings of a bigoted small town in the deep south. The locals do not like murder, but some of them dislike negroes even more. Nevertheless there has been a killing, and Virgil is a detective who has specialised in homicide. His temporary secondment is unpopular, at least initially, with the local police chief – but things improve as Virgil shows what he is made of, and solves the case in classic style.

Thus 'difficult' subjects are now being tackled in detective fiction, and John Ball's treatment of the colour bar gives his work added punch. Another author, James McClure, followed the trend and set his detective novels in South Africa. The detective, Lieutenant Kramer, is an Afrikaaner with a coloured assistant. His cases are modern versions of classical detection, but naturally the question of apartheid is one which even in detective stories it is impossible, as well as undesirable, to ignore. In the first Kramer case

McCLURE James
The steam pig
Victor Gollancz 1971

there is confusion at the undertakers in Trekkersburg because a post mortem is carried out on the wrong body. Moreover a wound is found, possibly made by a bicycle spoke, and Kramer investigates.

Although the books of Chester Himes are not in the classic style, he is mentioned here after Ball and McClure because again his detective is black. In fact there are two, Coffin Ed Johnson and Grave Digger Jones, who first appeared in

HIMES Chester B
Cotton comes to Harlem
New York Putnam 1964; Frederick Muller 1966

and made an immediate impact. Himes presents a mixture of humour and violence in a way that can not be compared with any other series of police novels. He is starkly realistic, at times appalling and at times sad, and his situations would be even more appalling if comedy did not occasionally intrude.

To return to Britain, the classical form was represented from 1959 by a writer who now has a substantial list of reputable works to his credit, H R F Keating. He exploded on the scene with several detective novels of an intellectual flavour, and yet they each had distinctive settings or other features which stamped them as extraordinary. For example in the first,

KEATING H R F
Death and the visiting firemen
Victor Gollancz 1959

a delegation from the American Institution for the Investigation of Incendiarism Inc are met at Southampton by a stage coach carrying a reception committee in nineteenth century costume. The farce takes a different turn, however, when a highwayman is shot dead.

Arguably his best detective novel is

KEATING H R F
A rush on the ultimate
Victor Gollancz 1961

which is set in a boys' preparatory school during the summer vacation, when the annual croquet week is to be held. This very civilised game was obviously well researched by the author, and we are treated to a description of the match. The players, however, are destined not to complete their tournament. For not only has a convict escaped from Broadmoor, but someone has found an original use for a croquet mallet.

Following several highly entertaining and skilful novels, Keating created his own series detective – Inspector Ghote of the Bombay police. Possibly the Ghote stories suffer a little by sometimes making the plots subordinate to the character, although it must be admitted that Ghote is a truly humorous creation. The varied settings also give us a chance to see the impact of a comic and none-too-efficient Indian detective on his surroundings, and vice versa. The standard varies considerably, but a particularly good Ghote story is

KEATING H R F
Inspector Ghote goes by train
Collins 1971

in which the inspector travels to Calcutta to collect a prisoner and finds himself indulging in a guessing game with a fellow traveller.

While on the subject of comic detectives, one must not forget the two really accomplished exponents of the humorous crime novel,

Joyce Porter and Colin Watson.

In Chief Inspector Dover, Joyce Porter created the most unspeakable character in modern detective fiction. Obese and idle, with his efficiency as a police officer constantly open to question, it is almost surprising that we can find him amusing. But Miss Porter has a deftly humorous way with words, and Dover muddling through is a piece of farce few writers can equal. His first case, aptly entitled

PORTER Joyce
Dover one
Jonathan Cape 1964

was followed by several others, but the joke began to wear a little thin. Miss Porter was equal to the occasion, and set us laughing again with a new character, the Hon Constance Morrison-Burke. In

PORTER Joyce
A meddler and her murder
Weidenfeld and Nicolson 1972

an Irish au pair is murdered near the Hon Con's residence, and that worthy lady tramples forthwith on another case. She is aggressively upper crust, with a hide like a rhinoceros and a tendency to bully the lower classes. In the Hon Con novels, Joyce Porter has combined first class detection with what is normally called black comedy.

Colin Watson, on the other hand, has built his comedy around a whole town rather than one central character. Behind the faultless facade of Flaxborough there lurk many feelings which are far from exemplary, and the principal citizens display more than a trace of hypocrisy. Colin Watson caricatures while managing to walk the thin line between comedy and farce. He presents detective puzzles to be solved, but does not intend them to be taken too seriously. Among his regulars, etched so admirably, are Chief Constable Chubb and the get-there-in-the-end Inspector Purbright. The Flaxborough novels can be thoroughly recommended, and the best introduction to them is

WATSON Colin
The Flaxborough Chronicle
Eyre and Spottiswoode 1969

which includes an introduction by Julian Symons and consists of *Coffin, scarcely used* (Eyre and Spottiswoode 1958); *Bump in the night* (Eyre and Spottiswoode 1960); and *Hopjoy was here* (Eyre and Spottiswoode 1962).

It will therefore be seen that the classic detective novel and the humorous detective novel have been well represented, separately and combined, during the past few years. Realistic police novels form another popular category, and we have recently seen fictional policemen at work in Holland and Sweden, as well as in Britain and the USA.

The novels which F R E Nicolas wrote as 'Nicolas Freeling', and which feature Van der Valk, are realistic in their acceptance of the fact that crime is a part of life. It is sometimes in the open, sometimes behind the masks of the respectable businessmen. Freeling does not dwell upon police procedure, although Inspector (later Commissioner) Van der Valk is so much more than a cipher. We can assess his relations with other officers, with his French wife Arlette, and with the characters with whom he rubs shoulders daily. If he must be denied a class of his own, he must rank with Maigret – we see Amsterdam through the eyes of Van der Valk as vividly as we see Maigret's Paris.

Nicolas Freeling, for a field like detective fiction, is unusually outspoken. His penetrating analysis leads us towards a more understanding view of social problems, and particularly those relating to crime. The first three Van der Valk novels were collected as

FREELING Nicolas
The Freeling omnibus
Victor Gollancz 1968

which consists of *Love in Amsterdam* (Victor Gollancz 1962); *Because of the cats* (Victor Gollancz 1963); and *Gun before butter* (Victor Gollancz 1963).

Two Swedish writers, who again are interested in the roots of crime rather than merely presenting a police documentary or whodunit, are Sjöwall and Wahlöö. A good example of their work is

SJÖWALL Maj and WAHLÖÖ Per
The man on the balcony: The story of a crime.
    Translated by Alan Blair
Victor Gollancz 1969

and they present the police force of Sweden in a somewhat disrespectful light. The early examples were sometimes grim with occasional light relief, but they have recently changed their style with

SJÖWALL Maj and WAHLÖÖ Per
The locked room: The story of a crime. Translated from the
    Swedish by Paul Britten Austin
Victor Gollancz 1973

This locked room murder mystery is a serious affair, with senior detective Martin Beck facing one of his most difficult cases. His colleagues of the Stockholm Police, however, are hunting a gang of bank robbers. The Special Squad, under the leadership of 'Bulldozer' Olssen are soon giving a passable imitation of the Keystone Cops. At what point, the reader wonders, will the two investigations collide? In the meantime we are treated to an extremely amusing adventure with Sjöwall and Wahlöö in a new mood.

Turning again to Britain, the police novel is still in capable hands. Roderic Jeffries, who writes also as 'Jeffrey Ashford', has produced some very worthwhile examples of the documentary type, although his policemen do not have to wrestle with as many cases simultaneously as, say, Gideon's men in the J J Marric series. Nevertheless it is clear that Jeffries has a working knowledge of the law and of police procedure, and his novels have shown a welcome degree of ingenuity. For example, in

JEFFRIES Roderic
A traitor's crime
Collins 1968

it is brought home to John Keelton, Chief Constable of Flecton Cross, that one of his detectives is 'bent'. But which one? An investigation begins, and provides us with a refreshing variation of the whodunit.

Another book, this time under the Ashford pseudonym, is a portrait of the life and duties of a country divisional detective inspector. In

ASHFORD Jeffrey
Investigations are proceeding
John Long 1961

there are several crimes at any one time within the jurisdiction of the DI. He has to have a finger on each, which is not easy. As with the Gideon books, an impression of authenticity without pretentiousness is conveyed.

Another writer of the British police novel, and one whose own service in the force ensures his adherence to the rule book, is John Wainwright. From the publication of his first,

WAINWRIGHT John
Death in a sleeping city
Collins 1965

we were introduced to the brutality of organised crime in a northern city. That city, or the country around it, has been the setting of almost every Wainwright novel since then, and he has been a prolific writer without a consequential lowering of his standards. He has a good

103

reputation and a large following, and the men of his city police force are by now well known to his regular readers. Some are tough, some are scared, but all are human. In his major work

WAINWRIGHT John
The last buccaneer
Macmillan 1971

the central character is Jules Morgan, a madman who claims to be a descendant of the pirate Henry Morgan. As his ancestor plundered, so Jules intends to plunder. He intends to plunder the city, and in an unusually long novel we follow the actions of the criminals and the police until the final holocaust.

The Wainwright novels are hard and tough, resembling Ed McBain rather than J J Marric. McBain, however, has another counterpart slightly nearer home – Elizabeth Linington, who uses the pseudonyms 'Dell Shannon' and 'Lesley Egan' in addition to her own name.

The three names of Elizabeth Linington are all labels for competent detective novels, mainly of the police procedural type, but the 'Dell Shannon' stories featuring Luis Mendoza and the Los Angeles Homicide Squad just have the edge. A good example is

SHANNON Dell
Murder with love
New York Morrow 1972; Victor Gollancz 1972

in which Mendoza and his team have a mixture of murders with which to contend, and an earthquake does nothing to help. In the Shannon novels we observe the domestic life of some of the detectives, and this creates a welcome contrast to the often grisly aspects of their day to day work. This combination, so popular with Marric and McBain, is an interesting feature.

No mention has been made so far of the 'hard boiled' school. Although several of the authors mentioned earlier produce works that are tough and incisive, the 'hard boiled' detective novel as a type does not seem as distinct as it was some thirty years ago. There are, it is true, dozens of wisecracking private eyes still to be found in the pages of modern fiction, but if we insist on a high degree of literary ability we can single out only one really first class exponent of the last decade – Ross Macdonald – and even he started over twenty years ago.

Kenneth Millar has written at times under his own name, as 'Ross Macdonald' and as 'John Ross Macdonald'. His novels featuring Lew Archer, the Los Angeles private eye, have been hailed by the critics as

something special. It was clear from
    MACDONALD John Ross
    The ivory grin
    New York Knopf 1952; Cassell 1953
that he dug psychologically deeper than his predecessors in the hard
boiled tradition. In this case Lew Archer is hired by a woman to find a
coloured girl who used to work for her, and who left with some ear-
rings and a necklace, but no case is ever that simple. Like Hammett
and Chandler before him, Macdonald uses the private eye to show the
dirt beneath the surface glitter of some parts of American society. The
later novels, labelled 'Ross Macdonald', are consistently readable.

Having considered the contemporary detective story and the police
novel, we are left with a wide ranging field. The detective novel cum
crime novel, as mentioned earlier, is a hybrid. Some are nearer to the
classic detective story, whereas others are psychological suspense
novels which are connected with the genre only because a crime has
been committed. A deliberate attempt will therefore be made here to
confine coverage to those authors whose works have a 'who?', 'how?'
or 'why?' interest rather than those who merely pose the question
'what will happen next?'

Firstly, there are some authors whose books have shown a transformation from detection or near-detection to the modern crime novel.
Dr Doris Bell Collier Ball, for example, has been writing for many
years as 'Josephine Bell'. From her series of detective stories featuring
Dr David Wintringham, which began in the thirties, she turned to
novels with an atmosphere of the sixties and seventies. This can be
clearly seen in
    BELL Josephine
    A hydra with six heads
    Hodder and Stoughton 1970
when the recently qualified Dr Cartwright is accused of the rape of an
unattractive patient. The same thing happened to the doctor for
whom he is locum, and who has since been found dead in Southampton Water. Cartwright becomes involved in a complex web of corruption, and the plot demonstrates Josephine Bell's success in
retaining the twists and surprises of conventional detective fiction
without its pre-war cosiness.

Evelyn Berckman similarly began with fairly straightforward
detection, although rather better than most. A good example is
    BERCKMAN Evelyn

A simple case of ill-will

Eyre and Spottiswoode 1964

where bridge club quarrels lead to the mysterious death of a member, but Miss Berckman has now diversified substantially in style and subject matter. Her most recent novels come into the suspense category rather than under the umbrella of pure detection. A particularly interesting example is

BERCKMAN Evelyn

The victorian album

Hamish Hamilton 1973

which tells how a latent medium, Miss Teasdale, is impelled by an old album she finds in her attic to delve back into the past. She is rather curious about a death which, it seems, had been swept well under the carpet.

Gwendoline Butler's series of detective novels concerning Inspector Coffin have been deservedly popular. In

BUTLER Gwendoline

A coffin from the past

Geoffrey Bles 1970

he investigates the death of Thomas Barr MP, concerning which salacious rumours are rampant. In a later work, however,

BUTLER Gwendoline

A coffin for Pandora

Macmillan 1973

the author abandons the inspector of that name, and presents a novel of suspense set in nineteenth century Oxford. She conveys the 'upstairs-downstairs' contrast of the rich and the poor, and presents us with a governess heroine whose life becomes at risk once she gets involved in a mysterious death and a kidnapping.

Another writer whose style has changed slightly is 'Ellis Peters', who is in fact the novelist Edith Pargeter. From fairly conventional detective fiction such as *Death mask* (Collins 1959) and *Death and the joyful woman* (Collins 1961), she turned to some detective stories with an Indian background. In particular,

PETERS Ellis

Death to the landlords!

Macmillan 1972

is a powerful whodunit derived from the fact that landlords are not beloved in India. Sooner or later brooding hatred gives way to murder, and on this occasion a party of young tourists become involved. One of them is Dominic Felse, son of Inspector Felse who appears in the earlier books of Ellis Peters. It is a well plotted whodunit, but its background and implicit social commentary makes it so much more.

A long career as a crime novelist has been enjoyed by Elizabeth Ferrars, whose straightforward and competent detection is exemplified in such works as *Alibi for a witch* (Collins 1952). Again a recent change of style, a keeping up with the times, is evident such as in

FERRARS Elizabeth
The small world of murder
Collins 1973

in which Nicola Hemslow accepts the Foleys' invitation to spend Christmas with them. The atmosphere is unlikely to be particularly happy, as the Foleys' daughter has vanished from her pram outside a shop, but Nicola hardly expects them to start accusing each other of murderous intent.

There is one other writer who must be mentioned in connection with the transformation from detective novel to crime novel – Paul Winterton, who writes as 'Andrew Garve'. Although he has rarely written the purely intellectual type of detective puzzle, his earlier books had much more of a whodunit flavour than those he has written during the late sixties and seventies. He is a remarkably versatile writer who ties himself down to neither a series character nor a recurrent central idea. For example in

GARVE Andrew
Boomerang
Collins 1970

we see a young city tycoon, in prison for dangerous driving, making useful contacts for pulling off an ingenious and hazardous plan. He needs at least £100,000 to conceal his embezzlement, and they all set off for Australia to put the plan into effect. But as the title implies, all is not straightforward.

In complete contrast is

GARVE Andrew
The late Bill Smith
Collins 1971

in which a successful salesman knows that someone wants him dead, and can only escape and discover the truth by disappearing on a 'permanent' basis.

To complete this survey of the sixties and seventies, five more authors will be considered. All are British, and none are writers in the

107

classic detection mould.

Firstly, the work of Harry Carmichael has remained of a high standard for many years. They can be categorised as suspense novels, although there is a strong detective element. Mr Carmichael's principal characters are John Piper, an insurance assessor, and Quinn of the *Morning post*. They specialise in finding themselves unwittingly in situations involving murder, and many of the books show how they extricate themselves and expose the guilty party. For example in a comparatively recent title,

> CARMICHAEL Harry
> Remote control
> Collins 1970

Quinn has a drink in a pub with a man called Hugh Melville, and slightly later a man is run down and killed by Melville's car. When Mrs Melville is found dead, and murder is suspected, Quinn finds the police are looking a little too determinedly in his direction. That is when Piper lends a hand.

Then there is Joan Fleming, another consistently good crime novelist over a long period. Although in

> FLEMING Joan
> You can't believe your eyes
> Collins 1957

she was fairly traditional in tone, demonstrating that four witnesses to a murder each saw something different, she later began to explore various themes and include something in the nature of social commentary. For example her smart doctor in

> FLEMING Joan
> Kill or cure
> Collins 1968

has his stamping ground in the 'gin-and-tonic or Jag-belt south of London', and the money flows freely enough for abortions to be arranged smoothly and confidentially. Comes a death, however, and Jeremy finds himself involved with a blackmailer.

Miss Fleming can be conventional or off-beat as the occasion demands, and she also demonstrates a neat contrast from time to time between the gruesome and the humorous. Her versatility is obvious, and she extended still further by producing a crime novel set at the time of the industrial revolution called *Screams from a penny dreadful* (Hamish Hamilton 1971).

'Anthony Gilbert', together with Carmichael and Miss Fleming, can be placed on the list of writers who have been turning out sound and professional crime novels for many years and yet never seem to get mentioned in the same league as Agatha Christie or Ngaio Marsh. Possibly it is because none of them have specialised in the classical puzzle, which of course was the favourite of readers until comparatively recently. Certainly their quality of writing, plotting ability and characterisation have all been of high quality.

'Anthony Gilbert', real name Lucy Malleson, has in fact never failed to enthrall and entertain with her stories of Arthur Crook, the unmannerly lawyer who is normally treading a narrow path between legal practice and the opposite. In

GILBERT Anthony
Is she dead too?
Collins 1955

he sets out to find a housekeeper who has dangerous evidence in her possession. Her employer has killed twice already, and is eager to find her before Crook does.

Twenty years later, Crook is still helping damsels in distress. The damsel in

GILBERT Anthony
Murder is a waiting game
Collins 1972

has been accused of the murder of her husband and cleared. Now, after ten years, a blackmailer is threatening to produce new evidence.

The novels of Laurence Meynell are slightly similar to those of Andrew Garve, in the respect that they often concern people who get progressively deeper into a desperate situation. Sometimes this is because of their own weakness, and sometimes because they deliberately set out to commit crimes. Among the best of the recent Meynells is

MEYNELL Laurence
A little matter of arson
Macmillan 1972

which shows two detectives investigating a case of arson in a south coast town, each with a different suspect in mind. Quite different is

MEYNELL Laurence
The fatal flaw
Macmillan 1973

in which two young members of the Chelsea set plan to carry out the perfect crime and then – like so many others – find they can not stop.

Finally there is crime novelist Dick Francis, whose books have been categorised as everything from adventure yarns to detective fiction. There is in fact a strong detective element in them, as they usually involve a crime and the hero needs to get to the bottom of it – to right a wrong, or to clear himself, or to expose the villain. Champion jockey Dick Francis, who retired from professional riding in the fifties, now has a long list of crime novels to his credit. His first one,

> FRANCIS Dick
> Dead cert
> Michael Joseph 1962

was immediately acclaimed, and followed by more with the world of racing as a backcloth. The dead cert of the title is an unbeatable horse – except that in this instance he falls, and his rider is killed. Jockey Alan York, who knows from the outset that a trip wire has been used, is determined to find the men responsible. This is a hazardous pursuit, as the gang will not hesitate to kill again, and it seems likely that their leader is one of York's friends or acquaintances. Unputdownable is an overemployed word in crime fiction reviewing, but this one – and in fact most of Dick Francis's books – are just that.

So this guide to the best detective fiction is now up to date. Not quite, because the novels of the past few years produced by new writers are impossible to place in their context. Suffice it to say that the detective story and the crime novel are both in good hands.

Among bright lights of the seventies, whose works will probably be listed as 'the best' in a few years' time, may be mentioned Catherine Aird, Marion Babson, Dominic Devine, Elizabeth Lemarchand, Peter Lovesey, Jessica Mann, Jennie Melville, Ruth Rendell, and Sara Woods. And when one remembers that many of the experienced practitioners mentioned in earlier sections are still producing new material, it is abundantly clear that the genre still has a deal of life in it. Or alternatively, to borrow a phrase from Mark Twain, any reports of its death are greatly exaggerated.

Checklist of books mentioned

111

DATE DUE